THE ART OF
SOUL WINNING

7 EFFECTIVE STRATEGIES TO WIN
SOULS IN THE SOCIAL MEDIA AGE

BRYAN C. JONES

DEDICATION

This book is dedicated to the God who loved me so much that He sent His Son Jesus to die for my sins that I might live. It is to God's glory that I dedicate this book. In addition, I dedicate this book to the first soul winner I've known, my mother Jo Ann. Thank you for allowing God to use you to save me and Daddy!

Next, I dedicate this book to the soul winner who works besides me every day and supports me, my wife Danielle.

Lastly, I dedicate this book to all the gospel preachers, soul winners and disciples who molded me, taught me and poured into to me that I might win souls. This book is dedicated to all of you. Thank you.

TABLE OF CONTENTS

Strategic Soul Winning Development

Strategic Soul Winning Discipleship

TABLE OF CONTENTS
(Continued)

Strategic Soul Winning Development

INTRODUCTION

It happened on October 30, 1974 in Kinshasa, Zaire (now the Democratic Republic of the Congo) between undefeated Heavyweight Champion George Foreman and former Heavyweight Champion and challenger, Muhammad Ali. The fight was called "The Rumble in the Jungle", and to this day, it is one of the most recognized and most watched fights in all of boxing history. The Champion, George Foreman, was known for his hard-hitting, heavy punching style and it made him a 4 to 1 overall favorite to defeat Muhammad Ali who was known for his speed, defensiveness, maneuverability, and tactical prowess. With so many knockouts to his credit, Foreman had proven all he needed was one perfectly placed power punch to do the same to Muhammad Ali.

During the earlier stages of the fight, Foreman began to cut off the ring to hinder Ali's mobility. As the fight progressed, Ali realized he would be unable to sustain the amount of energy necessary to escape Foreman's wild, ferocious punches. Consequently, Ali changed his strategy. He began to lay on the ropes, protecting himself from Foreman's violent punches. Ali allowed Foreman to wail away at him while he rested on the ropes. Shockingly, most of Foreman's punches never connected as Ali continued to lay on the ropes. Against the advice of his trainer, Ali continued this strategy to allow Foreman to tire by punching himself out.

Consequently, Ali changed his strategy.

1

Ali capitalized on this strategy in the 8th round when Foreman was exhausted and couldn't protect himself from an onslaught of punches. Ali managed to put together a flurry of punches that knocked Foreman out, rendering him unable to get up before the referee counted to ten. Muhammad Ali had regained the Heavyweight title to become the Undisputed Heavyweight Champion of the world for the second time! Ali's boxing genius introduced a unique strategy to the world that allowed him to gain victory over a difficult opponent.

The strategy Muhammad Ali used to defeat George Foreman is known as "The Rope a Dope", a strategy of allowing an opponent to tire out as the non-aggressor lies and rests on the ropes while protecting himself from potentially dangerous knockout punches. Ali was smart, tactical, and wise to use a strategy that placed himself in a position to win, even though the strategy he used to defeat Foreman wasn't advised by others since it wasn't what boxers traditionally thought of as a viable option to succeed. Muhammad Ali's mastery of the art of boxing was his ability to adapt to adversity by making strategic adjustments during fights to become victorious.

Forty-six years later, we find ourselves situated in acculturation in the Christian world where we are facing a much bigger and more powerful opponent than Muhammad Ali faced against George Foreman in 1974. We're facing a silent killer in the form of a global pandemic, and the knock-out punch coming at the face of the world is the Coronavirus which has claimed nearly 594,000 lives in the United States before the completion of this book.

Out of nowhere, the deadly punch of the Coronavirus hit the world so hard it decimated many churches and neutralized the effectiveness of their ministries. However, God is calling congregations of the Lord's church to adjust and use wisdom to develop strategies to win souls even during a painful and paralyzing pandemic. Ironically, what led Muhammad Ali to victory over George Foreman was his use of a strategy that was unpopular, unconventional, and unproven.

If the church is going to flourish in the biggest global fight of many of our lives, we must use the most effective strategies to win the souls of sinners and sustain the souls of the saved in the social media age. Openness to modern technological strategies which may have been unpopular, unconventional, and underappreciated in times past, could be key to keeping our ministries vibrant, viable, and victorious. This book is a guide to help ministry workers use the most effective and proven strategies to achieve spiritual success in a time where the enemy has delivered a knockout blow and decommissioned the mission of many ministries.

Making technological adjustments in the age of social media may not be the easiest thing to do for some, but if the gospel of Jesus Christ is going to thrive and not be thwarted by our current societal conditions, utilizing the most effective strategies to do so is key. *The Art of Soul Winning* could take your mission and ministry from micro to macro! In these pages you'll find a strategic, step-by-step approach to making the proper ministerial adjustments to save souls in the social media age.

Reasons for Utilizing Effective Strategies

It seems the salvific phenomenon of sinners giving their lives to Jesus Christ utilizing biblical salvation in modernity is becoming more challenging to witness in the church. As secular interest in our modern cultural climate continues to evolve, interest in Jesus and His word continues to devolve. For quite some time, church buildings increasingly appear abandoned as their older congregants age and the hope for a

> *The devil has managed to dismantle and demilitarize our evangelistic efforts to diminish the damage of sin.*

vibrant future for many churches seems bleak at best. Discipleship has been defunded in many religious circles that claim to be concerned about the eternal destiny of mankind. The devil has managed to dismantle and demilitarize our evangelistic efforts to diminish the damage of sin.

We now live in a world where the Great Commission given by Jesus Christ to His disciples has seemingly spiraled into a Great Descension. There has been a mass exodus of youth in many churches. Many of our young people and young adults are uninterested in the practice of Christianity as its potency and practice is less plausible during the pandemic. Although we have access to copious amounts of information in the technology age, we are raising a biblically ignorant (unaware) society where many congregations of the Lord's church continue to witness themselves experience a slow and painful death. Our current chaotic cultural climate has negatively impacted Christianity. The evolution of what the salvation of mankind looks like in the 21st century needs much prayer, discernment, dialogue, and discussion.

However, the good news is there is still hope! The church can regain her former exuberance, enthusiasm, vigor, and vibrancy and reach unprecedented, never seen before levels for Christ to save the souls of mankind! WE CAN rejuvenate churches so they can flourish and be attractive, vibrant, modern, contemporary, connective and spiritually healthy by implementing effective, soul-winning strategies in the age of social media. These nuanced technological strategies have proven that they make an enormous contribution to saving souls and reaching the masses for generations to come!

Therefore, we will only be able to grow biblically sound, spiritually healthy, and evangelistic congregations if we change two things, our mentality and our methodology. Mentality and methodology are two powerfully invaluable terms that will aid soul winners in the process of educating a new breed of disciples of Jesus Christ. Disciples in the social media age must be informed of the path needed to transform sinners in our changing social culture without compromising or ever-changing the infallible truth in the Word of God.

Mentality

"See, I am doing a new thing! Now it springs up; do you not perceive it? I am making a way in the wilderness and streams in the wasteland."
– Isaiah 43:19 NIV

God has a historical track record of being a God of movement and progression. Therefore, it was no secret that in 2020 and 2021 the body of Christ experientially realized God was indeed doing a NEW THING! Though the church is one and has many constituents who have enjoyed the comfort of doing THINGS (ministry) according to the ways of the past, a change has now come. We've learned that if the Kingdom of God is going to survive, thrive, and stay alive, we must adapt to a mentality of change! The word "change" can be frightening or even scary for many Christians since we live in a constantly changing world.

Ironically, change is a word we ought to be familiar with in the Christian world. Change is the very thing God demands we do as Christians every day to improve our moral behavior to conform to God's word, His will, and His way. (1 Thessalonians 4:1) Change is a necessary reality that we desire for those around us to implement when their change benefits us. However, many people find it hard to implement the very change they expect from others.

The world around the church is rapidly changing. Indubitably, present day churches fear losing traditions, congregational consistency, and the glory of the past. Perhaps some believe that the way things were in the glory days of the past is how God intends things to always be. Consequently, many churches are reluctant to change their mentality and methodology for fear of the unknown, the unproven, and the unconventional. This reluctance is to their detriment.

A large majority of Christians operating in modern culture have adopted modern ideas. Technological advancements and the cultural utilization of technology have become a way of life in our church member's households and workplaces. It would be strange, unattractive, unconscionable, and unimaginable for many people to accept entering into a non-culturally adaptive ministerial environment that is 30 years behind where the culture is trending now.

When considering familial impact, spiritually driven church families can powerfully contribute positive progressiveness in their church's culture. Among church families, there should be a variety of age groups in each congregation that provides a broader perspective of various mentalities that make up the church's overall dynamic. Utilizing the minds of multiple generations to impact the world for Christ through the avenue of modern methodology is a valuable additive to the church.

Methodology

During my senior year of playing high school varsity basketball, I'll never forget being overmatched when playing against very athletic opposing teams. Instead of using a one-on-one defensive strategy which exploited some of our weaknesses, our coach often switched our team's defense to a zone defense that hid our weaknesses. This allowed us to capitalize on our strengths and discover our opponent's weaknesses which enabled us to win. For soul-winning teams to win with the results of sinners being saved, we must understand our weaknesses and incorporate the best strategy and methodology, one that helps us become victorious.

Times have changed, but many churches have not adapted to a nuanced way of disbursing information that's congruent with the times. Decades ago, at the turn of the 21st century, the internet was launched. Since then, the internet has replaced libraries because of the vast amount of information that can be obtained through the internet. The worldwide web changed the game with how information is obtained and distributed. However, many churches to this day do not have a website to disburse information about who they are, where they are, and what they believe. Therefore, potentially interested persons who are geographically and technologically able to benefit from their ministries may be unaware of their ministerial existence.

The technology of the 21st century changed the process of how information was shared as well as how it was received. However, many churches continued to use the same communications channels as they always had instead of utilizing existing methodologies to aid in their approach to saving souls. Simply put, we need a STRATEGY, a PROVEN STRATEGY, to use what is available to reach those who need to be REACHED. The only question is, are you willing to change your MENTALITY and METHODOLOGY to win the souls that need to be won for Christ?

Even if you are not sure, I'm still extremely excited and elated that you are reading the words of this book! That first step means my prayer to God that he would use me to help strategically win the souls of mankind in the social media age has been answered! There's nothing I enjoy doing more than preaching, teaching, writing, testifying, and articulating the Word of God to assist in the process of sinners giving their lives to Jesus Christ. This book is designed to equip Ministers, Pastors, Ministry Leaders, and Christians of all ages with effective strategies that are conducive to saving lost souls in the age of technology and social media.

Revelation

The year 2020 was a historically challenging and unique year that continued to expose itself as a year of revelation; an amalgamation of devastation, salvation, and even creation. In the year 2020, life unfolded in a way no one could have predicted. The Coronavirus (Covid-19) decimated countries around the world and caused a global pendulum shift no one was ready for. For the first time, entire cities, states and countries were under lockdown orders to help stop the spread of this respiratory virus that hinders oxygen flow and thus restricts breathing capability. Hundreds upon thousands of loved ones were taken by this invisible virus. But the pain of loss from families throughout the world was clearly visible.

Initially, to protect the population from the virus, people were mandated by local and state officials to be isolated for months. Businesses closed, jobs were lost, hospitals were at capacity and, with the death toll constantly increasing, the salvation toll seemed to be decreasing. During this time most churches closed the doors to their buildings. Congregations no longer met physically to prevent the spread of the virus within their churches. Although there remains no cure for the coronavirus, after wreaking havoc on humanity for one year, a vaccine was released in the earlier part of 2021 to stop the spread of the virus.

As a result of the global Coronavirus pandemic, the world was forced to explore different technological forms of communication. The goal was to get information to the masses without physical contact but retain an informative impact. Many, if not the majority, of the churches in America began to use social media platforms to disburse messages which opened a technological pandora's box!

Though many larger churches had been utilizing television and social media platforms for years, churches and organizations that were novices to the online communication avenues were forced to communicate in unfamiliar ways. Many Christian constituents who abdicated against social media had no choice but to join social media and become acquainted with it. Otherwise, congregants would be forced to remain disconnected from their church's ministry because the options for physically assembling were non-existent or limited at best.

The revelatory unfolding of 2020 began changing the landscape of ministry during the height of the coronavirus impact as people began to realize that they were no longer able to use their normal methods of communication. The mass consensus for ministries whose goal is to provide life-changing messages was that they needed to use what was readily available. Now, a church with 50 to 100 members has the potential to reach people all around the world. Under normal circumstances, those individuals viewing a church's online messages would probably never enter their stationary buildings. Hence, the great commission Jesus Christ gave to His disciples seemed to come to virtual fruition after being birthed through a painful pandemic.

Global Impact

"And He said to them, "Go into all the world and preach the gospel to all creation."
–Mark 16:15

Although Christianity has experienced great omission from capitulating to the great commission of Jesus Christ to His disciples, much wisdom can be gleaned from the words of Jesus in Mark 16:15. The

Lord Jesus instructed His disciples of their vocation, "**go**", their location, "**into all the world**", their proclamation was "**preaching**", their preaching ammunition was "**the gospel**" and their destination was to reach "**all creation**". Contextually, this calling and commission were limited to the cultural forms of transportation available at the time.

I find it interesting that Jesus doesn't mention the specifics of travel, whether it be by boat, ship, foot, horse, donkey, buggy, train, car, plane, paper, or through the internet! Jesus didn't mention a specific methodology of how the preaching of the gospel could occur to reach all the creatures in the world, it was all fair game to accomplish their mission. Now God has given us a multimedia platform that will help us reach "all creation" from our kitchen tables, offices, cars, and stationary locations!

One of the best things that came out of the global pandemic of 2020 was the fact that God interrupted the routines of humanity. Everyone's regularly scheduled programming was placed on standby for what God was doing to command the attention of a planet that had ignored and avoided contact with the God of creation for quite some time. Christians now have access to an amalgamation of creative ways to communicate information from the word of God to an open, scared, and intrigued generation. Many hearts who are open to listening now would not have given any attention to life, death, or eternity if God hadn't intervened through the unfortunate nature of a pandemic that claimed many lives.

The reality is many people need an experience for God to get their attention. Don't forget the New Testament writer Paul said, "And we know that God causes all things to work together for good to those who love God, to those who are called according to His

The reality is many people need an experience for God to get their attention.

purpose." (Romans 8:28) This revelation of administering the gospel to hurting souls during a season of endurance was an opportunity for those evangelistically inclined to reach the masses through every form of available communication. Disciples who thirst to do ministry will always have opportunities if we remain focused on our calling to win souls for Christ even during times of grief and despair.

My Calling to Ministry

Many times I've been asked to explain how I was called to ministry and what that experience entailed. Technically, every Christian is called to ministry, but specifically, people want to know my path to the pulpit as a Preacher, Minister, Evangelist, and Spiritual Leader of God's people. So for the benefit of those who may want to know what makes me qualified to give this evangelistic insight, here is my attempt to glorify God by articulating what He did.

As a young man, I went through a period in my life where I indulged in a lifestyle of worldly living, satisfying my flesh, and I engaged in what I thought at the time was just having fun. The problem I wrestled with was the fact that I knew the truth of God's word and the right thing to do. I was raised in a Christian household where Christianity was practiced, and I had all the tools I needed to be Godly. However, I drifted back into the world after I was saved at the age of 18.

Through it all, I thank God for the Holy Spirit because as time went by, I became increasingly uncomfortable with who I had become, and I was unsettled with my status in the kingdom. I was sick and tired of allowing my flesh to win the battles over my behavior and mind. Something had to change. I was losing the battle of the mind and the hope of eternal salvation because of my worldly decisions. It was nobody's fault but mine. Finally, I had a similar experience to the prodigal son, I came to my senses and decided to go back home to Christ and become faithful to His church. (Luke 15:11-32)

From Sales to Souls

After years of reckless living, worldly capitulation, and spending many days and nights depressed because I failed to behave the way I knew God expected me to, I decided to truly repent from the practice of sin. I made a personal commitment to God and myself. In this commitment I made up my mind to walk the straight and narrow and refuse to compromise my spiritual integrity. I was determined to attend every service my church had because all I wanted to do was get closer to God and obey Him. I wanted to become completely surrendered to God and do everything I knew He wanted me to do. One day I attended an evangelism class. The instructor spoke about a very familiar Bible verse and explained the sacrifice it takes to reach lost souls for Jesus. It blew my mind because I was finally able to see the light in the passage of Mark 16:15-16 when Jesus told His disciples to "preach the gospel to all creation". It was a command, not an option.

All it took was to make up my mind to do what God said in scripture. I was shocked at how I had missed the necessity of applying passages of scripture into practicality all those prior years. Later in the evangelism training, the instructor discussed how being effective at evangelism requires being comfortable with cold calling, approaching strangers, and developing random conversations to engage the lost in conversation. As I sat there and listened, it dawned on me that the description and prescription being articulated on how to become an effective soul-winner was the exact description of everything I had ever been successful at doing in my secular career.

At that time I had been in the field of corporate sales my entire career and was a top performer, having received multiple promotions in my sales jobs. I was comfortable talking to strangers because that's what I was successful at doing on my job. I was comfortable persuading strange people and getting them to say YES because that's what I was trained to do in my job as a salesman. I was comfortable with developing relationships and persuading persons because that's what I was accustomed to doing on my jobs. I was comfortable with training and managing sales employees because that's what I did in my jobs.

When I looked back over my life, every job I had since my very first job as a teenager involved the skills I would need to win souls for Jesus Christ. At that very moment I felt a strong sense of confirmation about what God was preparing me to do with my life. From that experience, I knew ALL I wanted to do was focus on how I could help other people know Jesus Christ for themselves. I learned that God can use THE WORLD to TRAIN YOU, but THE WORD to TRANSFORM YOU! I became obsessed with sharing the gospel of Christ and I had a desire to devote every second I could to do what the Lord has commanded me to do as a disciple. Still, at this point, I wasn't thinking about being a Preacher, I was concerned about carrying out God's commission of preaching the gospel as my mission. My focus went from sales to souls!

I learned that God can use THE WORLD to TRAIN YOU, but THE WORD to TRANSFORM YOU!

I read the Bible for six to eight hours a day on numerous occasions. I tried to schedule and set up one-on-one Bible studies with anyone and everyone I could who would say yes to study with me. During this time, my Preacher became my mentor and I spent much time with him

13

in training classes doing ministry assignments and tagging along beside him doing ministry as I followed his lead.

On one occasion during this pastoral mentorship time with my minister and preacher, he attended one of my personal Bible classes at a student's home. After evaluating me, he gave me some valuable techniques, insight, and knowledge that helped me tremendously in the area of soul winning. Each week I scheduled multiple Bible study classes with individual students. I went into people's homes, I'd study with them over the phone, meet with them at the church building or restaurants, it didn't matter.

I was so purpose-driven to win souls I would meet any person anywhere to show them biblical salvation. I consistently began to baptize people from personal Bible studies for the remission of their sins. Sometimes weekly, sometimes two or three baptisms a day. I became so obsessed with winning souls that one day I had five different personal one-on-one Bible studies. As my influence began to grow within the congregation at the church I attended, my minister called on me more frequently for ministerial assignments to teach publically as well as preach.

Progression of Promotion

I developed a passion for helping the people in the pews through the Word of God without ever having a desire to preach publically. After baptizing dozens of people I was asked to preach a sermon on Sunday by my mentor and minister. I immediately said yes, although not because of my desire to preach, because I had no desire to preach. I was only desirous of being obedient to God and honoring Him while being faithfully committed to helping people. What was interesting about my preaching experience was that it was a natural progression in my ministry to do publicly what I was accustomed to doing privately. Through my ministerial experiences, I have since realized that it is dangerous to have a passion for publicly preaching in the pulpit without having a private passion for the people in the pews.

Many have a passion for the public pulpit because of the perception and perceived glamour associated with public preaching. However, they want nothing to do with the ministry assignment that takes place behind the scenes to strengthen the faith of God's people by helping them with their daily affairs. After my first sermon, I was convinced that not only did God want me to do a teaching ministry, but also a public preaching ministry. After that first preaching assignment I quickly received confirmation after confirmation from God of my life's calling and assignment to solidify the conviction of my calling.

Promotion

My first ministry assignment as a Preacher was a church plant in the neighboring state of South Carolina, my home state. I drove two hours from Georgia to South Carolina one way across state lines, back and forth weekly for almost two years. Notice how attractive this assignment was; we had no money, no salary (only paid travel expenses), no building, no following, and no pronounced presence to garner any influence with the local people. But what we did have was faith, and I read somewhere that if you have faith the size of a mustard seed you can move a mountain! (Luke 17:6)

In less than two years I witnessed God move us from no members in an unattractive classroom located in a poverty level zip code to a brick building in the heart of the city. We built relationships, canvassed the city, conducted one-on-one Bible studies and kept preaching. The

Lord started to give the increase. I was personally involved in countless evangelistic studies that led to many souls being baptized into Christ for the forgiveness of their sins.

During my first ministry assignment I witnessed how the Lord allowed us to grow from zero members to about one hundred souls who were baptized in just a few years of ministering in that city. However, the whole of ministry isn't all numerical growth, results, and joy.

For years, I not only opened and closed the building, I was also the preacher, song leader, prayer intercessor, counselor, janitor, trustee, treasurer, security staff and visionary in one person. That servile attitude was just my level of dedication to God. Besides, there was nobody else to do it.

There were many times in the infancy stages of that ministry when no one showed up for services, not even one person. I can remember the anxiety of standing in the doorway of our rented space, watching cars drive by on the street hoping each car would turn into the parking lot. Or two or three people would come after I'd worked on a sermon for twenty to thirty hours. This happened on more than one occasion. But I would literally preach to those two or three people like there was three thousand people in the room. Then I'd spend two hours driving back home and I'd think, pray to God and strategize. I learned when no one else is there to watch you, God is watching you. Therefore, I committed to DOING THE SMALL THINGS WELL because I knew God was always watching me. Even though we had many emotional disappointments during that time, I remained convinced God was taking us somewhere special. Many preachers probably would have quit, but I was confident that God had given me a gift that He wanted me to use despite the adversity and growing pains we experienced. I truly believed if people allowed me to use my gift to teach them about Jesus, I could help them improve their spiritual quality of life. I kept trying to save souls and improve on my ministry regardless of the results I saw when I first started.

Little did I know that in just three and a half years of preaching my first sermon, God would have me preaching the Word of God each week to 1.4 million homes on a local television station that was broadcast in three states. We stayed on television for almost five years on a shoestring budget. Thousands of people watched every week, donations came in and people wrote letters to thank us for the Word of God. During those years I co-produced every television show before it was sent to the television station. This production experience gave me valuable insight on presenting a ministry in the technological age to the public that I use even to this day in my current ministerial assignment.

The point in telling you this is not to brag about my positive experiences or depress you with my negative experiences. Rather, it's to help you see God moving in the life of a preacher who sought to win souls. I want you to see my heart as you read this book. I've put in enough work to have seen God do extraordinary things with someone called according to His purpose, which for me, is to seek and save those who are lost. The Art of Soul Winning is a book that will change the landscape of Heaven if those who love God will strategically band together to carry the gospel to a technological generation who is in desperate need of the Savior.

CHAPTER 1

STRATEGY #1: DEVELOP A PASSIONATE SOUL WINNING TEAM

To be successful in reaching the masses for the cause of Christ in the 21st century, every ministry needs a passionately charged team. Behind each passionate and compassionate soul-winning team, there must of necessity be a passionate leader. If the leader isn't passionate about the souls of mankind and making full proof of his ministry, there shouldn't be an expectation that people will follow his lead. As an Evangelist, one must believe deeply in Jesus Christ and His power to save lost souls through the gospel message. The purpose of the church is to save and sustain souls, but a purpose-driven church usually doesn't materialize without a purpose-driven leader. A purpose-driven leader has to be passionate about evangelism, passionate about people, and passionate about his beliefs in his work as an Evangelist.

Leaders who win souls must believe that people are lost and that they have the spiritual antidote to cure them from losing their souls and spending eternity in hell. If there is no burning theological belief that your labor is an eternally essential work recognized by God to change the landscape of Heaven, you won't put in the time, energy, effort, tears, or display of resilience to accomplish all you can for God. You have to be OBSESSED about doing all the good you can so that God can bless your efforts to impact someone's life spiritually.

It is of paramount importance to have a purpose-driven evangelistic leader for a soul-winning team to be developed. That development needs to be built on the premise of having visionary goals set forth by a visionary leader. People tend to follow what they see modeled. If the people of God can see the vision of winning souls, it can become attractive to them. Some will desire to be a part of it. Ministry teams must see the "WHY" behind the work ethic and leadership and see proven impact to get behind the cause of evangelism. If interested, soul-winning prospects can see the full vision of the leadership's evangelistic vision and direction, they could become great candidates for a cohesive team.

Picking Teams

I can vividly remember my childhood playground basketball days. In playground basketball, we had two team captains and each captain would pick who they wanted to be on their teams. As a team captain playing backyard basketball it was somewhat stressful having to choose one friend over another friend. But if you wanted an elite winning team, you had to evaluate your selection based on the strengths of the participants and what they could provide for your team to win.

By definition, a disciple is a learned follower. Disciples are individuals on the team of Jesus Christ who display discipline by distinguishing their demonstration of discipleship for the Savior whom they profess to follow. Congregationally, everyone who is a disciple should be responsible for spreading and sharing the good news as commanded by Jesus Christ. (Mark 16:15-16; Matthew 28:16-20) However, from a leadership perspective, assembling a team of purpose-driven individuals is paramount. These individuals are chosen because they have demonstrated the ability to help mobilize, stabilize and grow the evangelism ministry so that it can flourish with the salvation of lost souls as proof of their effectiveness.

Roles

To establish an effective soul-winning team for evangelizing the world in the age of social media, the right people need to be in the right roles. Roles on any team have to be established and adhered to. Much of the distractive drama that exists among teams materializes when people overstep their roles and take issue with things that aren't a part of their specific role. Organization and strategies are necessary for securing the foundation of a successful soul-winning team. Roles must be established and embraced by those who know their evangelistic roles so that the ministry of saving souls can operate in the highest spiritual capacity possible.

Social Skills

You need people who have the social skills conducive to being socially attractive in soul winning. For many people, the social phenomenon in the church of connecting to others is the initial primary influence before their participation becomes seriously theological and their interest is drawn to Jesus. I came to Christ through my social connection and the influence of my parents even after I was of age to think for myself. Through my social connection with my parents, I was placed in an environment where I was exposed to the preaching of the gospel of Jesus Christ. I went to church because of the social relationship and influence of parents, but after I listened to the preaching for years, I became theologically interested and informed of my obligation as a sinner through the information I received for myself. However, my relationship with Christ came to fruition first through my familial social relationship.

"and they were saying to the woman, 'It is no longer because of what you said that we believe, for we have heard for ourselves and know that this One is indeed the Savior of the world."

– John 4:42

The citizens of Samaria came to Christ based on their social relationship with the Samaritan woman who was impacted by a life-changing conversation with Jesus Christ. (John 4:42) Initially, the strength of the Samaritan's spiritual beliefs in Christ were largely embedded in the Samaritan woman's testimony of her acceptance of Jesus as her Savior. After the Samaritans got a chance to experience Jesus for themselves, no longer was the primary factor in their belief in Christ as the Messiah solely based on the testimony of the Samaritan women. The Samaritan's theological beliefs in Christ were substantiated by their own convictions and confirmations. (John 4:42)

The dynamic of developing nurturing social relationships with people is simply the initial connection that God uses to bring people into a relationship with Jesus. People with great social skills know how to leverage their friendships and influences to bring lost souls and loved ones into a theological atmosphere where they can be exposed to the soul-saving doctrine of Christ. People devoid of the basic social skills such as kindness, conversing, listening, smiling, loving, caring, sensitivity and being pleasant will run more people away from Christ than they will drive to Christ.

> *People devoid of the basic social skills such as kindness, conversing, listening, smiling, loving, caring, sensitivity and being pleasant will run more people away from Christ than they will drive to Christ.*

Many saints with good intentions haven't spiritually matriculated to possessing inviting and attractive social behavior to the lost. Spiritual behavior can become attractively inviting for sinners, but unspiritual behavior can be deterring for sinners to come to Christ. Without the right people, your soul-winning team could quickly become a soul-losing team if participants are not on the same page with the leadership and vision of the team. Therefore, ministry leaders must determine who has the potential to be a soul-winner or a soul loser.

A successful soul-winning team must be compiled of people who live with the spirit of excellence. Though imperfect, these people constantly seek to display Christ-like character. Soul winners must come to understand that everything they do can be used FOR THEM or AGAINST THEM when trying to lead souls to Christ. The strength of every ministry is never larger than the behavior its members either display or don't display. The success of any ministry is predicated on the spiritual character of its participants. If the leader is rotten, the rottenness of that behavior will trickle down to others and leave the group spoiled and corrupted. It has been wisely stated that if the leader is a clown, don't be surprised when his team becomes a circus.

> *It has been wisely stated that if the leader is a clown, don't be surprised when his team becomes a circus.*

I've learned to be careful placing people in ministry roles unless I've consistently witnessed their character and work demonstrated in some areas. There is an inherent danger in assembling a team of people to win souls if some believe in talent over character. If talent wins a person, that same talent won't sustain them. It's the character displayed that will either catapult a team or corrupt them. When selecting your soul-winning team and evangelism construct, it's prudent to choose CHARACTER over TALENT. Hopefully, God gives your soul-winning team both CHARACTER and TALENT!

Promoter Role

Every effective soul-winning team needs to have people with a spirit of promotion and preparation.

"The beginning of the gospel of Jesus Christ, the Son of God.

2 As it is written in Isaiah the prophet:

'BEHOLD, I SEND MY MESSENGER AHEAD OF YOU,

WHO WILL PREPARE YOUR WAY;

3 THE VOICE OF ONE CRYING IN THE WILDERNESS,

'MAKE READY THE WAY OF THE LORD,

MAKE HIS PATHS STRAIGHT.'"

– Mark 1:1-3

Preparing the Way

Before God sent His Son Jesus Christ to come on the scene in the flesh, it was prophesied through the prophet Isaiah hundreds of years before He came, that God would send a messenger to prepare that way. (Isaiah 40:3; Mark 1:2-3) The purpose of John the Baptist coming as that messenger before Jesus was to prepare the way of the Lord and make His paths straight. (Mark 1:1-3) Although God announced His coming hundreds of years before He came, the Father intended to use a man named John to prepare the hearts of the people to receive the Man, Mission, and ministry of Jesus Christ. John prophetically preached about the coming Christ and his message was for people to repent before Jesus came on the scene as the Messiah. (Mark 1:1-8) John's lifestyle was not a hindrance that impeded His prophetic message about the Savior.

The Voice

In the 21st century, John the Baptist would be similar to a marketing flyer, a video or commercial that advertises and promotes a product for consumption or use. In the art of soul-winning, people who will humble themselves to serve in the capacity of promoting the ministry are vital in leading souls to Jesus Christ. Every Evangelist, Minister, and ministry needs a John the Baptist. People like John the Baptist will help prepare that way by announcing something positive about their church, announcing the church's giftedness and their preacher's giftedness in efforts to lead souls to Jesus Christ! Yes, the more you use your VOICE to influence hearers concerning the mission and message of the preacher, the more hearts will turn to receive his message about the Messiah when they hear it. What's interesting about John's preparatory role as a messenger who came before Jesus is that his role required him to have humility.

John knew his role was to be out in front of the way, preparing the way! In ministry, disciples of God have to be humble, knowing their roles as Kingdom Promoter's to promote the ministry of saving souls. Regarding Jesus, John said, "He must increase, but I must decrease." (John 3:30) One of the problems with ministry teams is the lack of humility of those who desire to be a part of the ministry. John the Baptist knew that it was God's will for his role to diminish from where it once was, and John was okay with it.

Undoubtedly, one person will eventually be operating in a capacity where they will be seen visibly in the lights or camera more so than others. Some team members may become envious and jealous because their role isn't as visible as others so they shy away from participating in ministerial functions where they don't receive visible recognition, credit, or verbal praise. This kind of jealousy and envy can become a cancer among a winning team and destroy the ministry's effectiveness.

In contrast, John knew his ministerial responsibility was to play a lesser role to Jesus Christ and he was comfortable with that. This did not diminish John's gifts nor suggest his role was less significant than his previous role, but it says that accomplishing his mission to elevate Jesus was his privileged priority. Jesus said there was no prophet greater than John the Baptist. (Luke 7:28) Simply put, soul winners in the social media age must know their role is to be vocal promoters to give a path for the preaching and teaching of God's Word to shape and form the hearts of penitent believers.

Strategic Spiritual Recruitment

Jesus was extraordinarily strategic in the way He recruited disciples to work in ministry with Him. As you build a team of soul winners you have to operate strategically using those who possess the skill set needed for the work of saving souls.

"As He was going along by the Sea of Galilee, He saw Simon and Andrew, the brother of Simon, casting a net in the sea; for they were fishermen."
– Mark 1:16

Jesus was very observant. While walking on the sea of Galilee He saw two men, Andrew and Simon who were fishermen casting their nets into the sea. (Mark 1:16) Observantly, Jesus visually noticed both Andrew and Simon working on their secular jobs in the fishing industry. Interestingly, Jesus identified and sought after men with the

> *Interestingly, Jesus identified and sought after men with the pre-existing condition of a strong work ethic.*

pre-existing condition of a strong work ethic. Unfortunately, in contrast, I've seen leaders develop ministries with people who have no interest in putting forth the effort and commitment it takes to become successful.

Many churches start ministries with people who have never demonstrated desire or effort in the area of need, nor have they expressed any interest. But since it's the church, some leaders and ministry workers quickly desert skill, talent, and proven worth. This lack of leadership has disappointingly proven to be an unreliable strategy for effective ministry, especially the ministry of evangelism. No leader should expect the laziest, uncommitted person to suddenly demonstrate the most prolific work ethic to do the work required to minister to mankind. Leaders who observe the strategic nature of Jesus should become optically observant when developing dynamic soul-winning teams based on an individual's demonstrated performance.

Many disciples of Jesus Christ possess gifts within their secular careers that should be strongly taken into consideration when developing a soul-winning team or ministry. Unfortunately, gifts in the secular careers of church members are some of the most overlooked gifts that are commonly ignored by churches and ministry teams. In the secular careers of Andrew and Simon, we notice some important spiritual characteristics through their occupation of being fishermen. (Mark 1:16) Deeply embedded in the occupation of fishermen is a skill set that will aid Ministry Leaders in selecting a dynamic set of individuals who are committed to the ministry work of saving souls.

- Fishermen have to be familiar with fish.
- Fishermen have to be lovers of fish.
- Fishermen have to be patient.
- Fishermen have to be strategic.

- Fishermen have to be business-minded, possessing business sense.
- Fishermen have to be skilled in selecting the right bait for the right fish.
- Fishermen have to be persistent.
- Fishermen have to be experienced.
- Fishermen have to be acquainted with disappointment.
- Fishermen have to be dedicated to their craft.
- Fishermen have to be resilient.
- Fishermen have to be confident in their skill sets.
- Fishermen have to be familiar with the law of attraction.
- Fishermen have to be willing to put time into their craft.
- Fishermen have to be acquainted with the flaws of fish.
- Fishermen have to be aggressive in catching fish.
- Fishermen have to be knowledgeable of the geography in which fish reside.
- Fishermen have to be satisfied with fishing even when there isn't a catch.

If a strong team of soul winners is going to be constructed, an evangelistic-minded leader has to be keenly equipped with the skill of observation. Undoubtedly, there are usually people in every church that could have an enormous impact on reaching the lost if someone noticed that they possess a unique set of skills that could be useful in the kingdom. Winning souls requires patience, strategies, skill, persistence, experience, dedication, confidence, a strong work ethic, and commitment.

Leaders must know that God can transfer SECULAR SUCCESS into SPIRITUAL SUCCESS! God knows how to take the same skills, gifts, talents, and abilities He has blessed you with to develop on your SECULAR JOB and turn them into ministry! Remember, David the King experienced success as a shepherd who faithfully shepherded his earthly father's sheep, but was later promoted by God to shepherd over his heavenly Father's sheep. (1 Samuel 16:6-13) Paul, the talented theologian from Tarsus was a tent-maker by trade, who before ministry used his talents in the development of portable physical dwellings. After being called by God, Paul later used his craft to build permanent spiritual dwellings for sinners in the Lord's church as an Apostle, Evangelist, and minister of the gospel! (1 Timothy 1:12-17)

Jesus was a carpenter by secular trade and was familiar with using tools to build structures. In modern times a carpenter would be familiar with wood, hammers, insulation and nails used to create permanent structures. Isn't it amazing that God sent His only begotten Son, Jesus Christ on a mission using the skills He functionality developed on His secular job to accomplish His spiritual job as the Savior of the world? Jesus later built a permanent eternal structure known as the church of Christ when He was raised from the dead after three days! (Matthew 16:18)

Years ago, a good preacher friend of mine told me that in his past he used to sell drugs to make money before he found a relationship with Jesus Christ. He mentioned that he used to be a hustler, had connections, respect and possessed the gift of gab when he sold drugs. Since changing his life, he maintained the confession that even as a preacher, he still feels like a hustler, an influencer, and has the gift of gab! He told me all he did was CHANGE HIS PRODUCT! He's still a salesman, but he no longer sells DOPE. Now he sells HOPE! His SECULAR job undoubtedly prepared him for his SPIRITUAL job as a minister of the gospel of Jesus Christ. The same is true for anyone who desires to reach the lost for Jesus

Christ. Leaders must be able to identify the secular skills of potential team members which can be utilized in the spiritual realm of ministry.

The Importance Of Character In Soul Winning

Evangelism is certainly tough work, but despite the difficulty, nothing is more rewarding than planting and watering seeds for an eternal harvest. Soul winners must know that if you seek to win the souls of the lost to convert them to Jesus Christ, you will encounter some negative experiences. You will experience consistent rejection, defensive responses, ridicule, false accusations against your motives, accusations of being untrustworthy and dishonest, and people will attempt to besmirch your name in your efforts to thwart the proclamation of the gospel of Jesus Christ. There are many spiritual characteristics that soul winners need, so in this next section I will list a few characteristics that are of paramount importance when it comes to constructing a team of dedicated individuals that every church ministry needs to impact growth.

Faithfulness

A few years ago I was blessed to preach for a congregation of the Lord's people in Gary, Indiana, the hometown of legendary pop star and singer Michael Jackson. After the worship service, naturally, my wife and I had to go see where Michael Jackson grew up. When we visited his birth home, I was shocked at how small the Jackson's home was considering the size of their family. This encouraged me. I realized that big talent can originate from small and humble beginnings! It

I realized that big talent can originate from small and humble beginnings!

taught me that God PREPARES BIG THINGS IN SMALL PLACES! The size of where you are NOW is NOT AN INDICATION of where God is going to TAKE YOU through your HARD WORK. Never share your BIG DREAMS with people

> *Never share your BIG DREAMS with people who have SMALL MINDS.*

who have SMALL MINDS. Too many dreams and plans have been ASSASSINATED before they were ACTIVATED.

Some of you reading this book have started ministry from small beginnings. Even now you are confined to small places. Please know that God is PREPARING YOU and DEVELOPING your gifts in those small places! After the Lord elevates you, people will be SHOCKED when they find out how small the place you came from was. That will be your OPPORTUNITY to give God glory! Work hard no matter where you are right now and know your season of GROWTH and OPPORTUNITY is not coming, it is already here! The longer it takes you to see the results you desire, the more POWERFUL your TESTIMONY will be. The soul-winning strategies in this book will encourage readers who are struggling and frustrated because God currently has you where you are. Stand still and remain FAITHFUL. Your harvest will come, but it depends on how faithful you are at planting and watering seeds!

In the development of soul winners, there must be an understanding in each individual that this work requires a distinguished degree of discipline in the area of faithfulness. The essentiality of being faithful to the Lord Jesus Christ whose sacrifice saved you is the foundation of soul winning. Displaying faithfulness in the Word of God not only sustains you, it strengthens you. There will be times when no one else knows the effort you put into saving a soul from eternal condemnation. Remember, the same God who sees what you do in PRIVATE will reward you in PUBLIC.

Soul winners must understand that there will ALWAYS be people who desire to MAGNIFY what they don't see you do and be SILENT on the myriad of things they do witness you doing! When a spirit of criticism and hatred exists in the hearts of people, some will only SEE what they want to SEE or what they CHOOSE to SEE. Those of you who are serious about your calling must never get discouraged and deterred when people MAGNIFY what they perceive as your weakness.

Be confident in knowing your REWARD is going to come from a God who sees all that YOU DO publicly and privately. As your weakness visibly becomes a STRENGTH in the eyes of those who criticized you, God will REWARD YOU in front of the very people who seek your DOWNFALL and they will STILL REMAIN SILENT because people are by nature fickle! When God gives the increase from your labor, the God who rewards you and recognizes your faithfulness will get all the glory!

Soul winners have to possess a belief that their work is to help unsaved people understand the plight and purpose of Jesus' sacrificial death. Your efforts will be worth it when those whom you save appear before God as a Righteous Judge in the judgment. What Jesus Christ says in Matthew 7:21 becomes a powerful motivational reality that emerges from the text to aid in our soul-saving mission.

Doing God's Will

"Not every one that saith unto me, Lord, Lord, shall enter into the kingdom of heaven; but he that doeth the will of my Father which is in heaven. 22 Many will say to me in that day, Lord, Lord, have we not prophesied in thy name? and in thy name have cast out devils? and in thy name done many

wonderful works? 23 And then will I profess unto them, I never knew you:
depart from me, ye that work iniquity."
– Matthew 7:21-24 KJV

In Matthew 7:21, Jesus makes a startling declaration concerning the claims of those who would verbally profess Him as Lord. Jesus sadly announces that the deeds conducted in His Name by some of those people will not help them gain entrance into the kingdom of heaven because those deeds were not according to God's will. (Matthew 7:21-24 KJV) Doing God's will is the key underlining principle for those in the kingdom of heaven to strive for. Contextually, these false, self-serving religious leaders and evil-doers professed Jesus as Lord, a term of authority, but Jesus professed to them that their deeds were not in the will of His Father in heaven. The point is that soul winners must truly believe that people of all walks of life, religious people, and those without a relationship with God MUST do His will found in the Bible.

To expect an eternal destination of Heaven, one must believe that God's Word is the authority that dictates and determines our actions and behaviors. The art of soul-winning involves believing that no matter how or what people have proclaimed to have DONE to solidify and secure their relationship with God, His Word is the ultimate authority for our salvation, beliefs, righteousness, practices, worship, and spiritual activities. We must have faith that God's Word is what propels our actions regardless of what mankind says or believes.

Despite what the majority of like-minded individuals say, no matter what scholars, academicians, and theologians say, obedience to God's will is what we believe allows us to enter the kingdom of God and the kingdom of heaven! No matter whether it's a family member loved one, friend, or philosopher, God's will in His Word gives us our marching orders. Our faith must lie within God's will. Nothing more, nothing less.

Commitment

In every relationship, there must be a commitment to the principles, values, and morals that make relationships mutually beneficial and successful. The relationship between Jesus Christ and Christians is no different. The love for the Savior and His commands should drive dedicated disciples of Christ to a commitment to soul winning. The work of evangelism requires observation, articulation, inculcation, and spiritual motivation, knowing Jesus Christ is pleased with your work. (2 Timothy 4:5)

If you scarcely receive the acknowledgment or credit for your efforts to reach people for Jesus Christ, your mindset should remain satisfied with being a seed planter. It has been widely articulated that if you live for compliments, you will die by criticism. The motivation of a soul-winner's commitment happens when Christians are faithfully committed to the Word of God and the reality of mortality. The reality of our mortality should lead to concern in responsively marrying lost souls in Christ. The longevity of life isn't always a reality, but eternal comfort lies within the Christological reality of salvation by faith in Jesus Christ. (Acts 2:47; Galatians 2:16; Ephesians 2:8-9)

At any time, Jesus Christ could return to His church. Those who have obeyed His gospel and remained faithfully consistent with God's will during their lives will enjoy a pleasant and peaceful eternal destiny. (2 Thessalonians 1:6-10; Revelation 2:10) The reality of humanity's mortality is simply the fact that after death, mankind will either have a pleasant resurrection in Heaven or an unpleasant resurrection in hell being in eternal condemnation. (Matthew 10:26-28) When people die, many will realize that they lived lives contrary to God's will while being congruent with their own will.

That reality will unfortunately occur for many souls, and they will be lost in eternity. Then these lost souls will realize that God was the One and Only True God. They will remember that God was a loving God who demonstrated His loving-kindness to humanity by sending His Son Jesus Christ for the atonement of the sins of humanity, but they failed to believe in Him while they lived on earth. Unfortunately, people who ignored the sacrificial atonement of Jesus for the forgiveness of their sins while they lived on earth will burn in hell and suffer forever because of that decision. (Revelation 21:6-8; 2 Thessalonians 1:6-9) If there is someone you personally know who doesn't live life according to God's will and they have failed to understand this eternal reality, you ought to do something about it.

Knowing You Have Eternal Life

"And the testimony is this, that God has given us eternal life, and this life is in His Son. 12 He who has the Son has the life; he who does not have the Son of God does not have the life. 13 These things I have written to you who believe in the name of the Son of God, so that you may know that you have eternal life."
– 1 John 5:11-13

Soul winners must develop the confidence, belief, and knowledge that we have eternal life in the Son of God. (1 John 5:11-13) Disciples should mentally remain in a constant state of motivation to help others gain access to the same process of salvation God has provided us through faith in Jesus Christ. (Galatians 2:16) John helps us become fully assured that we can KNOW we have eternal life, as God Himself wants us to KNOW it! (1 John 5:11-13) Once we have obtained a relationship with the Son of God eternal life becomes our reality! (1 John 5:11-13)

As Christians, we know this and are motivated by the beauty of our salvific reality. We know there will be a time when the way we conducted our mortality as mankind will matter and this should motivate us to remained saved and save the lost. Soul winners must be committed to doing all they can so that every person has an opportunity to develop the same spiritual conviction. Obeying the Savior of the world and continuing our beliefs in the Son of God will solidify eternal life for all born-again believers. (1 John 5:11-13)

Submission to Leadership

"Obey your leaders and submit to them, for they keep watch over your souls as those who will give an account. Let them do this with joy and not with grief, for this would be unprofitable for you."
– Hebrews 13:17

For there to exist a team of faithfully committed individuals who have God's mission as their mission, there must be an attitude of submission among them. No teams are perfect, but in the Lord's church we don't always value the commodity of submission as an expression of obedience and loyalty to the mission of God. (Hebrews 13:17; James 4:7) The reality is that as Christians, we are all human. We all have ideas and things we believe would work better strategically and logistically.

Often, the potential to secure the most effective and gifted ministry and evangelism ministry teams becomes thwarted by Satan's demonic influence. Soul-winning efforts are dissolved because there isn't always an agreement by individuals on these teams with the logistics of how the strategy is to be implemented. For example, some people abort the mission when they disagree with the strategy or plan of the mission and thus discontinue their involvement in the ministry altogether.

35

But it doesn't stop there. These individuals will try to convince others not to be involved either because they disagree with the strategy of the leadership in carrying out the mission. Countless individuals have left ministries because they didn't agree with the selected implementation of the strategic plan adopted. While they agreed with the mission, they refused to engage in submission to leaders who strategically planned the mission.

Submission is important because no one will agree with everything that everybody does. But it isn't only submission to the mission that is important. It's also important to submit to the leadership God has positioned to carry out His mission. Submission is being faithfully committed to the mission when YOU DON'T AGREE with the strategy or its implementation.

"Let not many of you become teachers, my brethren, knowing that as such we will incur a stricter judgment."
– James 3:1

The preacher is a man of God. The preacher is God's man and God has given him the vision that sometimes others cannot see. (2 Timothy 3:16-17) For example, the preacher, the evangelist, the man of God is not some ordinary man equivalent to everyone else in role functionality or even God's judgment. (James 3:1)

The man of God is distinctively different because of his ROLE. The man of God is different and holds a higher charge, more responsibility, and his job description, as well as responsibilities, are giving by God, not mankind. (2 Timothy 3:16-17; 4:1-5) The question becomes, will those who are faithfully committed to the mission of saving souls understand that God has charged the man of God and church leaders with the responsibility to spiritually equip the members to do the work of service?

(Ephesians 4:11-13) God's desire is for His people to exercise submission when in disagreement or agreement with the path chosen or strategy of the leadership. Never allow the turbulence of the ministry to cause you to jump overboard from the mission and fail to land safely at your desired destination.

Leaders Must Equip the Saints

"And He gave some as apostles, and some as prophets, and some as evangelists, and some as pastors and teachers, 12 for the equipping of the saints for the work of service, to the building up of the body of Christ; 13 until we all attain to the unity of the faith, and the knowledge of the Son of God, to a mature man, to the measure of the stature which belongs to the fullness of Christ."
– Ephesians 4:11-13

Christians must not only submit to the mission of saving souls, but also to the leaders whom God has chosen to implement His work. The cohesion and chemistry of the church's mission of saving and sustaining the lost will have what it needs to flourish when this occurs. Submission is a concept that isn't the easiest thing to do, but without it, teams will not achieve the righteousness of God and develop into all God has for them to become. Commit to exercising submission in your mission that it may aid you in being a progressive, cooperative, faithfully committed member of a soul-winning team that God has

Faithfully submit to Godly leadership and KNOW YOUR ROLE!

designated to populate Heaven. Your submission could be the permission God requires to promote you! Faithfully submit to Godly leadership and KNOW YOUR ROLE!

CHAPTER 2

STRATEGY #2: DEVELOP AN ATTRACTIVE SOCIAL MEDIA PRESENCE

A few years ago I spoke with a gentleman who explained to me how he had recently installed a new energy-efficient HVAC (heating, ventilation, and air conditioning) unit in his home. He articulated to me all its benefits and how much money he saved through the installation. From there our conversation moved into how the advancements of technology had positively changed so many things in the world for the better. Then he decided to tell me a story about his six-year-old daughter who had been adversely affected by technology.

The gentleman told me that his mother was babysitting his daughter at her house. She asked her granddaughter to turn off the lights several times. Each time the grandmother left the room she heard her granddaughter playfully clapping as children do. But every time she came back into the room expecting the lights to be turned off, they were on. Her granddaughter repeatedly failed to listen. Finally, when the grandmother came back into the room for the last time and the child still hadn't turned off the lights the grandmother decided to punish her for her blatant disobedience. In tears, the six-year-old granddaughter said, "I tried to turn off the lights, but they wouldn't go off!"

It just so happened that the girl's dad walked into the house to pick up his daughter just as his mother was about to punish her. When the young man realized what was going on, he explained to his mother that he and

39

his daughter live in a smart home where their lights operate on a sound sensor. At home, his daughter simply claps her hands together and the sound activates the lights to turn them on and off. Ironically, up to that point in her life, his daughter had never learned anything about turning lights on or off in conventional homes. So, what the grandmother thought was disobedience, was only an understanding of current technology without any knowledge of older conventional technology.

Personal Preference

I shared this story because there is an entire generation of people who need to be saved but were born and raised during the technology age and that is all they know! In the area of soul winning, to exclusively approach those people with only one form of communication is to possibly ignore their preferred method of communication for the sake of our preferences. If ministry teams are going to be effective, we must communicate and share information not only inside a building, but also through a variety of methods that are germane to how this generation communicates. You can't attract a 21st-century TECHNOLOGICAL AUDIENCE with a CASSETTE TAPE APPROACH!

You can't attract a 21st-century TECHNOLOGICAL AUDIENCE with a CASSETTE TAPE APPROACH!

Let's be honest, the preferred method of communication of many young people and the masses in the 21st century is through the avenue of technology, particularly social media. I know that many people and churches have struggled with the notion of rationalizing and accepting social communication through technology, but it's here to stay and it's not going anywhere! When Jesus asked His disciples to go into all the world and preach the gospel to all creation, He didn't exclude various methodologies (social media platforms) to get the job done even though they weren't around during His time. (Mark 16:15)

I strongly believe that face-to-face social interaction in the physical setting is indeed the best way to communicate. However, while acknowledging this reality, I also understand that one video of the word of God being preached at the right time in a person's life is important. So is the fact that one video can reach more people around the world than one message preached in a brick and mortar building can. In addition to assembling in one physical location, developing an attractive social media presence is an aid to getting the word of God out to people outside of the building setting. There is no limit on how many people you can reach unless you limit your communication avenues.

Social Media Presence

Cell phones, laptop computers, iPads, iPods and digital software used to create video footage content has become the norm. People communicate through Facebook, Instagram, Twitter, Snapchat, YouTube, TikTok, Podcasts, blogs, and a host of social media venues that allow them to share pictures, videos, and short messages. Many say they aren't interested in joining social media because of the negativity. Some have a fear of the unknown. I get it, I used to believe the same thing years ago before I joined social media.

A few things changed my view of social media. For starters, I was fearful of social media and thought that someone could hack my personal information and people could say nasty things about my social media presence, so I didn't want to put myself at risk. I assumed the worst about social media and chose not to get involved with placing positive spiritual information on social media. I was wrong. Social media has privacy measures to protect your account from unwanted people or posts, so having that knowledge cured my social media fears.

Secondly, I didn't want to be negatively influenced by the foolishness and drama I'd heard from my friends that people display on social media, which made being on social media sound like a waste of time. But God showed me that I wasn't on social media to become influenced by anyone. God wanted me on social media to become an INFLUENCER! God had given me a way to access and influence more people online than I would ever see inside a building. If I wanted to save sinners, and there were millions of them active on social media, then I needed to go into the world of technology where I could reach those who needed Jesus.

"And He said to them, "Go into all the world and
preach the gospel to all creation."
– Mark 16:15

It's interesting to look at our modern approach to ministry in comparison to the first-century disciple's approach to ministry in antiquity. Traditionally, we have focused on getting people <u>inside a building</u> to teach them the gospel of Jesus Christ. Consequently, many soul winners know how disappointing it feels to be unable to get people inside the physical church building to win their souls. When we invite the lost to a public assembly and they don't materialize, THE WORLD DID NOT COME TO US! It's as though we forget that Jesus did not say, "WHEN ALL THE WORLD COMES TO YOU, PREACH THE GOSPEL." Jesus said, "GO INTO ALL THE WORLD AND PREACH THE GOSPEL!" (Mark 16:15)

Please understand that I truly believe in the spiritual power of the corporate physical assembly of the church and inviting people to become a part of a community of believers! In-person fellowship will always be my preference. There isn't anything like being together as a church family hearing the word of God and fellowshipping in the corporate physical assembly. The social construct of physically assembling is desperately needed and a benefit for the saints of God. (Hebrews 10:24) All Christians should fully appreciate the surpassing value of having a church building to congregate in, conduct meaningful ministry and enjoy the experience of edifying corporate worship.

However, we must not fall victim to believing the assembly of the saints in a building is the only or best way to reach lost people for the saving of their souls. I find it nothing short of amazing how social media has given us a way to spread the gospel of Jesus Christ through technology to get the Word of God into the hearts of sinners and those who need to be encouraged through their trials, troubles, tests, and tribulations.

The Shift

Years ago, when I used to work in the banking industry, I had a conversation with a business owner who owned a small landscaping business. This gentleman was old-fashioned and liked his clients to pay him with cash and good checks. I asked him if he had he ever considered accepting debit and credit cards to receive payments and he quickly said he wasn't interested. Then I asked him if he knew how many consumers use debit and credit cards to make purchases because they earn Rewards Points.

I explained that some consumers may not have cash or checks because they prefer to use debit or credit cards. Also, I told him that some consumers would also use credit or debit cards when they had emergencies or were just short on cash flow. This was something he hadn't thought about before. I helped him see that if he didn't consider using technology, he would simply be hindering the ways that people could pay him for his services. He realized his preference to receive payments may not always be the preferred payment method of his customers. Ultimately, he concluded that his stubbornness in refusing to adjust to considering other payment methods could reduce his income and limit his opportunities.

To relate this story back to soul winning, our past preferred methods of communicating the gospel of Jesus Christ may not be how all sinners want to receive that information today. For many people in the technological age, the preferred method is online through social media. The question is, what do you do when your ONLY preferred method of communication is antiquated, outdated, and not the preferred method of those to whom you are desirous of attracting to Christ? Of course, we intend to marry people into the congregational setting, but to initially reach them, we must have a variety of methodologies to do so.

As it relates to winning lost souls for Christ, God never intended for the gospel of Christ to be barricaded exclusively inside a building. We have been guilty of gospel confinement instead of creating new opportunities to fulfill our gospel assignments. As disciples, we limit our exposure and enslave the gospel of Christ to a building location if we **ONLY** use the building method to spread it. Scripture is clear that God intended for disciples to bombard the hearts of those who are broken with the gospel of peace. (Mark 16:15-16; Ephesians 6:15) We have to win souls by any gospel means necessary!

> *We have been guilty of gospel confinement instead of creating new opportunities to fulfill our gospel assignments.*

Visual Content

God has shifted the playing field in the ministry of saving souls. If congregations of the Lord's church plan to be effective in saving souls and communicating the gospel, you cannot miss this shift just because the current method hasn't been a past or previous preference. The shift is here and it's here to stay. We have to adapt to using the additional methods through which our culture expects to receive information. Below are a few things we should consider if we plan to win souls by distributing our biblical content in the social media age.

- Visual content is powerful.

- Visual content is strategically designed to connect humanity to reality.

- Visual content is helpful in conveying a message relatable to the human experience.

- Visual content has no expiration date.

- Visual content is useful for people with social anxiety disorders that arise in the physical assembly experience worship service.

- Visual content is attractive when it is creatively designed.

- Visual content is attractive when it is progressively designed.

- Visual content is attractive when it is impactfully designed.

- Visual content is attractive when it is engaging to its viewers.

- Visual content enables those who are sick and shut in to view the message of truth.

- Visual content is effective when there is a global pandemic.

- Visual content is not a replacement for physical assembly. (Hebrews 10:24-25)

- Visual content is an aid that captures what takes place in the physical assembly.

- Visual content is a way to reach outside of your building locally, nationally, and globally.

Social Media Visual Essentials

We are living in an age where the gospel has the bandwidth and elasticity to travel to realms unknown throughout the world. Yes, that same old-time gospel has the wings to travel to the remotest part of the earth as Jesus Christ prophesied to His apostolic witnesses before His ascension to be with His Father. (Acts 1:8-10) This same gospel can travel to areas in Indonesia and villages in Africa. The gospel can travel all the way to Hawaii, Alaska, and across the United States of America. It starts with a vision of believing that God can take the message of Jesus Christ from your spirit of humility to places beyond your imagination. Let's explore a few things every ministry needs to effectively disburse the Word of God in the social media age to win souls for Heaven's roll call.

Lighting

In 2021, social media consumers are conditioned to view and watch video content on television and the internet with all the bells and whistles that visual attraction offers. The visual quality and attractiveness of video content is impacted by lighting. It doesn't matter how good the content, sound quality camera resolution is if the people who have access to your video content can't see it! NO MATTER HOW GOOD IT IS, people in this generation may not give your video content a chance IF THE LIGHTING IS BAD. It is not necessary to spend thousands of dollars on equipment, particularly if you don't have that kind of budget. However, it is a priority to have good lighting for your video content to be taken seriously. The notion that lighting quality isn't to be taken seriously suggests a lack of vision and fails to position your ministry in the best social media light to express the message of Christ you are attempting to explicate. The online market is flooded with thousands of churches doing live streaming. Many of these ministries have a long-standing reputation for having engaging video content for their messages, so make yours as good as it can be by paying attention to lighting.

As people press play on your video, it is estimated that you only have about three to five seconds to get their attention, so be sure those first few seconds contain attractive, high-quality visual content. There are many ways to enhance the visuals with editing, lighting and graphics, but in the age of high definition and 5k resolution, people's eyes are spoiled and accustomed to visual royalty. People want movie quality clarity in the content they view, and it's that kind of attractiveness that may very well hold their attention long enough to hear the message you want to convey. Light it up!

Sound

Excellent sound quality for the listener when viewing video content increases the effectiveness of your audio and visual content. Unattractive sound erodes a person's focus and hinders their attentiveness to what is being conveyed or displayed. No one in the 21st century watching your ministry online is going to sit through a baby crying at the top of their lungs, miscellaneous conversations being heard in the video or any other background noise not intended to be conveyed. Sound will make or break the connection with a viewer, and poor sound quality will frustrate them to the point of ignoring your content.

Sound is very important in spreading the gospel in the social media age. If emphasizing the gospel is the primary objective, your message needs to be articulated in an attractive manner rather one that contains distortion or distractions. A good sound technician who understands the differences in various microphones and updated sound technology is essential to developing sound that is crisp and caters to the volume of the speaker. If the gospel message of Jesus Christ is going to be heard by the masses in the technological age, the sound quality could either attract them, or turn them away.

Camera

Cameras are an interesting phenomenon that has changed over the last few years with the explosion of high-resolution camera phones. In the 21st-century, cell phones offer high-quality resolution that gives a crisp picture and video quality on the same level, in my estimation, as expensive high-quality video cameras. With good lighting and sound as first cousins to your visual attractiveness, a high definition, high-resolution camera with 4 or 5k is certainly the route to go. Something engaging takes place when a camera has great resolution. Viewing content is much more attractive as viewers get the feeling that they are physically there. If a soul-winning ministry is going to share its content with the world, having multiple camera angles and/or software that switches angles is paramount to creating dynamic visual content for consumers.

The next time you watch television, pay attention to the number of camera angles you see in a show, movie, or commercial. You may find that those camera angles you never paid attention to is what kept your attention all these years as you watched television. Notice the time span between different camera angles. Most cameras switch to another angle after three to seven seconds which is the optimum amount of time to hold your attention. The utilization of multiple camera angles produces higher connectivity between the audience and the content and provides an in-depth view of the visual content. Whether viewers know it or not, the constantly rotating camera angles offer an anticipatory effect that becomes attractive to viewers.

Sometimes our spiritual content does not draw the viewership we desire. That outcome may not always be because of how interested viewers are in the content. It may be because the visual content doesn't hold a person's attention if they are accustomed to viewing the content from multiple angles which makes them less likely to want to view just one camera angle. The whole objective of the gospel message is to save souls, however, factors that affect the quality of the message make a difference in whether the content will be viewed and received. Camera quality, editing, video production details, and engineering can make or break your opportunity to get the word out to the entire world in this changing social media and technological age.

Content

It is not wise to have a Ruth's Chris gospel in your possession but then distribute it with a McDonald's level of service. As a preacher, I am keenly aware of how important content is to present the word of God to the world. As soul

> *It is not wise to have a Ruth's Chris gospel in your possession but then distribute it with a McDonald's level of service.*

winners and disciples of Christ, we know that the gospel of Christ is the power God uses to save humanity (Romans 1:16), but how that gospel is disbursed can be the determining factor on whether a person receives it in the social media age. In the western world, we now live in what I call the USA, the United States of Acceptance. Though we have access to much information through technology, many people choose to accept anything in religion as valid truth before verifying its biblical validity.

In generations past, people grew up in biblical homes where the Bible was believed to be the roadmap to God and Heaven. However, that is no longer the case now. The Baby Boomers and Generation X groups are now confronted with a staunch nuance of generational differences with those in the Millennial and Generation Z era. The Millennial (Gen Y) and Generation Z age groups may not have all been raised in mainstream Christian households like those in the eras before them. Consequently, these individuals may be unfamiliar with Christianity and the necessity of having Christ in their lives.

For soul winners, knowing the necessity of preaching Christ isn't the issue. Rather, it is how do we communicate the content of Jesus Christ to people in terms of where they are in their knowledge and understanding of this precious, Palestinian Jew named Jesus Christ. The message of Jesus Christ won't change, but the methodology may need to change if those in the soul-winning business are going to bring Jesus to the world. To be successful in the social media age we must figure out how to package Jesus to them in a way that is relative to their current social construct and human experience.

Relatable Content

People are impacted by spiritual content when the content speaks to and/or is relatable to a specific need in their present human experience.

Connections are formed when spiritual content hits the heart of those dealing with arduous and tumultuous situations. When biblical and spiritual content is used to bring awareness and share the message of Jesus Christ to creation, in my experience and through the feedback I have received, it should be inclusive of the following:

IDENTIFY | Biblical content must *identify* with the human needs of people and speak to those needs from God's biblical perspective. Only Jesus can supply the spiritual needs of sinners and social solutions to injustice through God's righteous justice.

EDIFY | Biblical and spiritual content must *edify* people with relevant biblical encouragement through passages of scripture. Jesus Christ is the only answer to the plight of humanity. (John 14:6)

SANCTIFY | Biblical content must explain the biblical distinction between God's covenant people and others in the world. Those in a *sanctified* relationship with Christ must learn about their uniqueness as subjects in God's kingdom.

GLORIFY | Biblical content must be given with applications to apply God's word. The *glorification* of God occurs when information leads to application, application leads to salvation and salvation leads to transformation. A transformed life is credited to God which leads to His *glorification*. (Matthew 5:16) We praise God for His transformative ability!

Social Media

Simply put, people connect with audio and visual content because they desire **inspiration** that is relative to the human experience DAILY! In the social media age, it's more than just the connection to social media that draws people's attention. If the content grabs their attention, they can focus on the depth of the content. If they focus on the depth of the content, the God of Heaven knows how to open their hearts to respond to the things spoken by the man of God. (Acts 16:14-15) Think about the times we live in. Most people are constantly on their phones and other electronic devices through which they receive and share pertinent information. Technology is one of the ways people communicate information. This is not to say technology is the only way, but undoubtedly it is for many in the 21st century.

While there are others, two of the most popular platforms to view video content are Facebook and YouTube. Any platform that offers video content allows anyone to watch 24/7. The reality is that most, if not the majority of these platforms are frequented by people in every church. If church members can access these platforms for social and secular use to influence their friends and family with content unrelated to spirituality, they have the power to use that same social influence on these platforms for God. The Facebook and YouTube platforms offer a wide array of attractive ways for soul winners to disburse appealing spiritual content to the hearts of those who are seeking help with navigating through this journey called life.

Remember, technology is only an aid for us to release real, relevant, and righteous truth in the Word of God to the world. The primary role of soul winners is to strategically plant the seed of the word into the spirit of people who need to hear it through all avenues. If the Kingdom of God is going to transact kingdom business, we must be like the men of Issachar who understood the times. (1 Chronicles 12:32) Lastly, if we are going to reach people communicatively on a level that honors God, we must learn to treat people with love, kindness, joy and respect when eagerly putting forth our evangelistic efforts.

STUDY GUIDE

MINISTRY WITHOUT WALLS

Let's explore a New Testament ministry construct that many Ministers of the gospel have done an excellent job of teaching, but many have never seen the fruits of their teaching applied functionally or completely grasped by those whom they taught.

In understanding that evangelism is a ministry without walls, a powerful question to contemplate is where does real ministry (service) originate? If this question is answered from a narrow view, it has the power to limit ministry to a specific geographic location. However, the real ministry must originate in the heart of an obedient disciple with an unfailing desire to please God and save souls. When Christians know their purpose is to seek and save that which is lost as Jesus Christ did, their purpose will never be limited to a location. (Mark 10:45)

During the global pandemic of 2020, we have learned much about ministry. One of the things we learned is that we live in a virtual reality. We were forced to worship and conduct ministry practices in unprecedented ways that we never did before. Although the physical assembling of the masses is our preference, we KNOW that ministry and even worship can take place OUTSIDE THE CHURCH BUILDING when the building option isn't available.

There are differences and similarities between ministry taking place *inside the church building* versus *outside the church building*. Certainly, both approaches are preferred, plausible, and possible. Let's explore some of the similarities and differences in the spiritual activities inside a church building versus outside a church building. More so now than ever, we need to teach the youth, young adults, aged and the elderly the VALUE of learning how to conduct effective ministry in more ways than just inside the church building context!

ACTIVITIES INSIDE THE CHURCH BUILDING

- We assemble to worship God in Spirit and Truth. (John 4:24; Hebrews 10:25)

- We are ministered to. (Hebrews 10:23-25; Romans 10:17)

- We study the Word of God together. (Acts 20:7; Romans 10:17; Ephesians 3:1-12)

- We fellowship with the Saints. (Acts 2:42)

- We pray with the Saints. (Acts 2:42)

- We commune together with the Saints (break bread). Acts 2:42; 20:7)

- We preach the gospel. (Mark 16:15-16)

- We stimulate one another to love and conduct good deeds. (Hebrews 10:24)

- We imitate Christ. (Ephesians 5:1; Romans 12:1-2)

- We demonstrate love for our families. (John 13:34-35)

- We demonstrate loves towards disciples. (John 13:34-35)

- We feed the hungry. (Matthew 25:42)

- We invite strangers. (Matthew 25:43)

- We clothe the naked. (Matthew 25:43)

- We mourn with the bereaved. (Matthew 5:4)

- We serve humanity. (Matthew 23:11)

- We spread the gospel by any means necessary. (Mark 16:15-16)

ACTIVITIES OUTSIDE THE CHURCH BUILDING

- We worship God in Spirit and Truth. (John 4:24; Hebrews 10:25)

- We are ministered to. (Hebrews 10:23-25, Romans 10:17)

- We study the Word of God. (Acts 20:7; Romans 10:17; Ephesians 3:1-12)

- We pray. (Acts 2:42)

- We commune (break bread). Acts 2:42; 20:7)

- We preach the gospel. (Mark 16:15-16)

- We imitate Christ. (Ephesians 5:1; Romans 12:1-2)

- We demonstrate love for our families. (John 13:34-35)

- We demonstrate loves towards disciples. (John 13:34-35)

- We feed the hungry. (Matthew 25:42)

- We evangelize strangers. (Matthew 25:43)

- We clothe the naked. (Matthew 25:43)

- We visit the sick and imprisoned. (Matthew 25:43)

- We mourn with the bereaved. (Matthew 5:4)

- We serve humanity. (Matthew 23:11)

- We spread the gospel by any means necessary. (Mark 16:15-16)

- We suffer for the cause of Christ. (2 Timothy 3:12)

Except for socially and physically assembling, Christians do many things inside the building that can be done outside of the building in ministry. The goal of this exercise to express the need to do ministry constantly, both inside and outside the church building, together as the Saints of God. Before the global Coronavirus pandemic of 2020, I would estimate that 95% of ministry in most churches took place *inside a building*. In contrast, 99% of Jesus Christ and the disciple's ministry took place *outside of a building*. Make no mistake about it, we love our buildings. We need them and yearn to assemble to fellowship among one another to enjoy the social dynamic of the body of Christ. However, **we must see the difference in being "ministered to" inside the building, versus "ministering to" persons outside of the building**. Some souls WILL NEVER come to your building unless you MINISTER to them outside your building!

Read Mark 5:21-43; Luke 5:27-32: In your understanding of scripture, did Jesus and His disciples conduct the majority of their ministry efforts inside a building or outside of a building? Explain the rationale of Jesus.

_____

_____

_____

_____

What has this lesson taught you?

_____

_____

_____

Is there anything you plan to do differently as a result of this lesson?

_____

_____

_____

_____

Discuss with another Christian how both of you can apply this lesson to your lives. Share your discussion below.

_____

_____

_____

_____

APPLICATION: Let's minister to people both inside and outside of the church building by demonstrating love, kindness and truth as the church should. Spend each day using the opportunities God gives you to show persons how to come to Christ using all methodologies available.

CHAPTER 3

STRATEGY #3: SHARE THE WORD ON SOCIAL MEDIA

In August of 2019, we witnessed the cataclysmic release and rise of the brand-new chicken sandwich at Popeye's Louisiana Chicken. Amid its release a chicken sandwich war was sparked from online internet comparisons between taste testers comparing Popeye's chicken sandwich to Chick-Fil-A's chicken sandwich.

The Lord used the Popeye's versus Chick-fil-A chicken sandwich debate to launch a powerful ministry affirmation into my spirit. As human beings, we love to use talking points. We like to celebrate, brag and discuss in detail how GOOD something we have experienced is. It's satisfying for some people when they can announce to others that they have experienced something great and grand! We know bragging makes other people crave to experience what we bragged about!

Wouldn't it be amazing after church if Christians left worship service and Bible study excited and happy to tell their friends how GOOD the SERMON or the Bible lesson was? What would happen if every Christian bragged and discussed the details of what they LEARNED about Jesus to their friends and family who don't have a relationship with Jesus Christ? What if saved persons bragged about their religious experiences to the degree that other people would want to desperately visit your church because of how you celebrate the teaching and how much God's word has TRANSFORMED your life?

Maybe our churches would then have lines like Popeye's Louisiana Chicken and Chick-fil-A, not because of the chicken, but because of their hunger for Christ. This will never happen if people don't brag and celebrate the doctrine of Christ and the transformational change they've experienced within their respective congregations and fellowships.

Super Spreader Events

The Coronavirus pandemic of 2020 taught us the danger of attending large social events where people refused to wear masks and physically distance themselves. These unfortunate occasions proved to be events where the coronavirus could spread on a mass level. These events were called Super Spreader Events. Contrastively, in events when God's word is being proclaimed, Christians should participate in both physical and virtual Super Spreader Events. When soul winners share the message of the ministry to save souls, even our online events could turn into super spreader events.

Though it's never been easier to share the word through any other avenue like it is with technology, at the same time, it's never been harder to get some people to do it. For some it appears to be easy, but for others it's the hardest thing to do. Sharing can be done with just the click of a button on our cell phones. Pressing a button sends a video of a sermon, spiritual devotion, debate, worship service, testimony, or Bible study on social media to friends and the world!

The word of God is the seed, the primary ingredient that God uses to save, but how that seed gets into the mind of the hearer is up to the people of God when SOUL WINNERS share the word! Communication takes place when information is accurately transferred

> *Communication takes place when information is accurately transferred from one mind to another.*

from one mind to another. Therefore, when the word that originated from God's mind and was recorded in the pages of inspiration (the Bible) enters into sinner's hearts, God's word is planted. The process of evangelism takes place when we share the good news through our kingdom's efforts. A powerful, paramount, and poignant ladder that leads sinners from the valley of sin up to the mountain of salvation is built when the gospel is SHARED on social media in the technology age!

For those who have active social media user accounts such as Facebook, it is important for the Christian to conceptualize and concretize the reality of what you decide to share. I cannot tell you how many times on Facebook and Facebook Messenger (a private messaging platform associated with Facebook) people have asked me to share videos. I've been asked by friends, family, and fellow Christians to share recipes, politics, personal pictures of family, traveling excursions, news clips, political jargon, personal videos of all these things in the secular world that cannot get anyone to Heaven.

Many Christians have adopted and adapted to sharing information in the social media age, but some fail to understand that they have excluded their own professed and proclaimed spirituality in their sharing process. YES, many Christians share more political and secular propaganda than they share uplifting soul-saving messages on social media. Meanwhile, the biblical messages from their church's ministry miserably fail to reach their friends. Therefore, if technology isn't being utilized as a tool to influence sinners to be saved, Christians are missing out on opportunities to persuade the masses. SHARING THE GOSPEL MESSAGE of Jesus Christ on every platform possible is the most powerful way for a child of God to get the gospel to their circles of influence!

There are three areas soul winners can SHARE the message of truth both theoretically and practically in the social media age. Disciples of

Jesus Christ and members of the Lord's church must *share the word*, their *witness*, and their *wisdom*.

Sharing The Word

One of the most effective ways to convert sinners in the social media age in the year 2020 is by sharing the word through relational connections. During the global Coronavirus (COVID-19) pandemic of 2020, I learned much about the benefits of social media and evangelizing the lost in this age. After it became our primary option once we closed the doors to the church building, members of our congregation shared the word of God via the Facebook platform. We asked them to invite those whom they knew relationally to watch online and worship with us. God opened the doors of the hearts of our congregants and visitors to hear the word of God in a spirit of desperation because people were hungry for answers and sermonic solutions from God's word.

Many people outside of the body of Christ began to listen to the word because members of our church shared the word of God with them on social media platforms. Some of these people heard the word of God for the first time in the pandemic with a renewed sense of seriousness that only God could have provided amid a changing and dying world. People who listened began to ask questions as if they were hearing the word for the first time.

In addition to sharing the word of God on their social media platforms with their respective circles of influence, many members watched our services online together with their family members and friends who were not Christians. For the first time, God began to get the attention of humanity because so many people were searching for answers, looking for spiritual clarity, and questioning their own mortality after seeing thousands die because of the Coronavirus pandemic.

One Sunday morning during the Coronavirus pandemic just before I was about to step on the stage to preach a sermon live on Facebook, I received a message from a lady on our church Facebook page requesting to be baptized. This woman had been encouraged to watch and listen to the sermon by her friend who was a member of our ministry. We were able to connect with her the same day and invited her to come to the church for a brief Bible study. After the physically distanced Bible study and gaining a better understanding, she immediately decided to become baptized into Christ for the remission of her sins.

So what caused the growth? How did this woman come to know Christ through a virtual worship service? It was a move of God, but it developed and materialized through a social relationship with a faithful friend through the avenue of social media. This lady's salvation story culminated with a one-on-one face-to-face Bible study where she received the courage, confidence, and conviction to say YES to Jesus Christ! The word of God was transmitted through the avenue of social media and the one-on-one Bible class produced a soul being won for Christ during a pandemic. Throughout this book I will candidly share more powerful examples of how to bring salvation to sinners in the social media age by soul winners committed to populating Heaven and depopulating hell.

Share Your Witness

It becomes quite clear when studying anthropology that human beings are attracted to what other human beings place value on. Therefore, what humans devalue, other humans will follow suit and devalue as well. I can remember growing up hearing conversations that friends were having about the release of the new Air Jordan sneakers. The Air Jordan shoes came with a high price, high expectations and high anticipation. Kids talked about how attractive the new Air Jordans were, and the conversations were very intense and convincing. If you didn't intend to purchase the new Air Jordans after hearing these conversations you felt like an outcast, someone not among the cool, elite, accepted crowd.

However, if you purchased the new Air Jordans you were automatically placed into a category in the minds of other kids as being someone special. People acknowledged you for taking pride in your appearance and wearing those shoes became an event, a statement-maker of who you were. I understand as we mature from children to adults that rationale and peer pressure sounds trivial, immature, and self-absorbed. The point I'm making concerning humans is that we speak so confidently, persistently, and convincingly as it relates to persuading people about purchasing products that possess no spiritual value. But we are silent when it comes to persuading people about Jesus who purchased our salvation with His own blood!

How is it that we have not placed the appropriate spiritual value on the preaching of Jesus, but we have placed value in everything else, thus devaluing the most important message of eternal significance? The art of soul winning is very much about persuading people to believe and trust in the same God who saved us the same way we received salvation from the scriptures.

People are consumers. What we talk about the most becomes persuasively consumable if we testify and become witnesses to others of what the Lord has done in our lives. What if we shared our salvation story about how Jesus Christ saved us and changed us in the same convincing way we talk about sports, music, art, and things with secular interest? Soul winners must view themselves as witnesses to what God

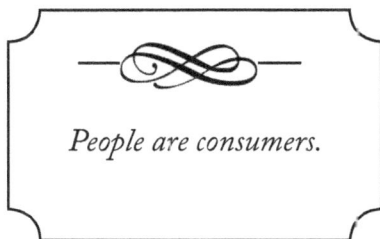

People are consumers.

has personally done for them. Articulating the beauty of your salvation testimony to sinners in a way that demonstrates how much value you have placed into God's plan of salvation is convincing. Do you know how convincing, important, and persuading it is for sinners to hear your powerful conversion story as a real witness to the power Jesus Christ has demonstrated in your life?

People Need Spiritual Help

Jesus cast out an evil spirit from a demon-possessed man who needed help. (Mark 5:1-17) The evil spirit caused this man to dwell in the tombs. He screamed day and night, gashing himself with stones, albeit while being naked. Sadly, this man remained mentally out of his mind and unable to be bound by chains due to his strength. (Mark 5:1-17) What's disheartening about this man's condition was his ability to use physical strength to break the chains, but he lacked the mental capacity to escape the realm of a spiritually damaging lifestyle.

This demonic spirit kept the man in a perpetual state of mental bondage. His mind was kept in solitary mental confinement while being demonically tormented. Though the man had issues with his pneumatology, sociology and dwelled in disturbing geography, for his condition to change, he needed to believe in the Master's theology. After Jesus demonstrated His power over the evil spirit using the spoken word, the formerly demon-possessed man was found sitting down, clothed, in his right mind with his behavior under the influence of God's Spirit. Then, the man implored the Lord to accompany him on His next journey. (Mark 5:18)

"And He did not let him, but He said to him, "Go home to your people and report to them what great things the Lord has done for you, and how He had mercy on you."
–Mark 5:19

In Mark 5:19 we notice that instead of following Jesus after his exorcism, the Lord forbid the formerly demon-possessed man to accompany Him. (Mark 5:19) Instead, Jesus instructed him on an assignment to become a news reporter. The man was to go home to his people, to those who presumably were familiar with his previous condition and give a spiritual transformation report to them! In his report, the Lord instructed him to tell the people what great things the Lord had done for him and how he experienced mercy, an elimination of misery.

There is a powerful principle in the Mark 5:19 passage as Jesus transformed the man's life so that he could become a witness to the transformative power of Jesus. A witness could testify from personal experience of the mercy and goodness of God by verbalizing what the Lord had done for them. What if born again, forgiven believers readily and routinely conducted spiritual reports to their families after the Lord transforms them? Many people are hesitant to communicate with their family after they have been born again for fear that they will be judgmental and question the legitimacy of their new Christian path.

Interestingly, as of first importance, Jesus wanted the man to go home to his family. This is an important principle for soul winners to understand. We should go directly to those with whom we have an existing social relationship. Those who know our past and would be shocked that the crazy person who was once out of their mind is now sober, clothed, in their right mind, and behaving because of a relationship with Jesus Christ!

As a child of God, you are a witness to how Jesus Christ has transformed your life. That itself may be the most impactful testimony you have. Your testimony doesn't have to involve much Bible knowledge at all. Jesus didn't ask the man to go home as a perfect man and quote scriptures. Jesus asked the man to "report" the goodness and mercy he experienced at the hand of the Lord from his personal experience. In other words, share the truth of your experience. Share the bad and how it culminated in an experience with Jesus that changed your life forever! (Mark 5:19)

Proclamation of Transformation

"And he went away and began to proclaim in Decapolis what great things Jesus had done for him, and everyone was amazed."
– Mark 5:20

Jesus was aware that the details of the formerly demon-possessed man's testimony would pay enormous spiritual dividends to those who knew him before his encounter with Jesus. This transformed man's obedience gives the soul-winner much insight into adding salvific value to a person's life through personal testimony. In Mark 5:20, the gospel writer Mark records the word "proclaim" as the man faithfully responded to Jesus' instruction. The word "proclaim" comes from the Greek word "kerusso" which is defined as a person who is a "herald", one who preached and proclaimed only what was ascribed to him by his master. Nothing more, nothing less.

It's also interesting that the transformed man was sent by Jesus to proclaim his testimony to the Decapolis, a region of ten cities. The Decapolis is a compound word comprised of "deka" meaning ten and "polis" meaning cities. The ten cities in the Decapolis were Scythopolis, Hippos, Pella, Gadara, Dion, Gerasa, Canatha and Raphana, and Syria (Damascus and Philadelphia). Jesus knew that when this man proclaimed his testimony that ten cities of shocked hearers were going to be impacted by what they heard and saw!

The brilliance of Jesus's request allows soul winners to understand the power of one man's testimony, one women's testimony, one sinner's testimony! One testimony of God's goodness and mercy impacts lives! If your testimony is proclaimed honestly and earnestly, it could impact many demographics and geographic locations of sinners who need Jesus just as badly as we need Him. Christians MUST be motivated to SHARE our testimonies! The power of the testimony isn't solely in telling it, the power is in God's transformative power to do what we constantly fail to do for ourselves.

Only God can change those who can admit they were out of their mind before meeting Jesus. Though you may not have been naked in the tombs, some of you reading even now can admit that there was a time in your life when you were naked, not in the tombs, but the college dorm rooms. Naked in some apartment, naked in some car, naked in some woods, naked in some house where you ought not to have been! You were out there naked! Some of you could equally testify that before God came into your life you had an evil spirit that controlled your behavior.

That spirit may have not been a natural neurological disorder, but your evil spirit came from drinking alcohol (spirits) and other substances that altered your mind. Thus, many of you know what it's like to have a spirit altering your behavior and causing you to be out of your mind, screaming at parties, screaming at people, screaming at the top of your lungs at sporting events and games! So you experientially know what it's like to be in submission to an unholy spirit in contrast to being in submission to God's Holy Spirit.

If believers would allow the Lord to change our hearts to become open to the enormous impact of sharing the message of Jesus Christ, lost individuals would be amazed at what the Lord has done. Sinners would become convicted once they knew that if the Lord could do those things for us, He could do those things for them. Soul winners need humble hearts to become unashamed witnesses who desire to share their testimonies.

One area of concern that hinders the impact of the gospel is when believers who are expected to be transformed do not behaviorally conform to the instructions of Jesus. When that happens the behavior is reported as untransformed to those who know us, which weakens our witness. The key isn't to live perfectly as only Jesus could, but to demonstrate that you live an improved, transformed spiritual life because of your relationship with Jesus. That will be enough for those who knew you pre-Jesus to see the post-Jesus improvement in your life.

Share Your Wisdom

"Wisdom is the principal thing; therefore get wisdom: and with all thy getting get understanding."
– Proverbs 4:7 KJV

The proverb writer instructs us that wisdom is the principal thing as its acquisition is paramount to obtaining understanding. Wisdom leads its occupants to live a lifestyle of making Godly choices which are a reflection of God through our behavior. (Proverbs 4:7 KJV) Wisdom is different from knowledge in that knowledge is the culmination of receiving information, but wisdom occurs when one is skilled and sophisticated at living. Wisdom knows if, when, why, and where to apply information functionally to increase God's desired outcomes for humanity.

When sharing the message of truth or testimony of God's merciful goodness in hopes to encourage sinners to receive Jesus Christ, we must use wisdom. It is also equally important to share the benefits of using practical wisdom in the age of social media to improve one's quality of life. It's not always about quoting Bible verses that people may not understand to condemn their behavior. People don't typically learn from Bible verses you quote; they learn from Bible verses you explain. Many times you can share Bible wisdom without giving any indication of the origin of the actual Bible verses you derived your wisdom from to help others live their lives. Below are two easy and effective ways God can use every active Christian to become a soul winner in sharing the word of God in the social media age.

Sharing Sermonic Wisdom

I'll never forget when I began incorporating the Bible wisdom I learned from listening to sermons in the church into my conversations with friends, family, and with people in my work circle. It's simple. If you are paying attention, you can always find a window of opportunity during a conversation once someone brings up a situation, problem, or issue they are struggling with. I would use sermonic wisdom just by articulating how to potentially solve or handle issues based on the knowledge I was accumulating from my minister's sermons during that season of my life. People began to look at me differently. They started to come to me for advice and ask for my thoughts before they would make decisions in their lives.

I had become a spiritual confidant, a mentor, and a trusted adviser to many people just by sharing the wisdom I learned from the Sunday sermon and Wednesday Bible studies I attended. I hardly ever used Bible verses, I simply shared the Godly wisdom I acquired through common conversation. Eventually, someone would ask me where I gleaned my information from. Those opportunities gave me a chance to share the source of how I obtained the wisdom God had given me. Sharing sermonic wisdom gave me credibility and a window of opportunity to invite people to the source where I received my knowledge. Many people began to accept invitations from me to come and hear for themselves what I was learning from my weekly worship service experiences.

From those experiences I learned when people find their source of wisdom, some become interested in obtaining that same wisdom after discovering how easily obtainable it is. If Christians SHARED their sermonic wisdom in conversation with their family, co-workers, and friends it would make a world of difference. There is value in acquiring sermonic spiritual information if you have a biblically thorough teacher of God's word. The key is sharing the sermonic wisdom and being unashamed to release it practically through the art of conversation. Sharing sermonic wisdom only works when you pay attention and take notes from the sermons you hear weekly through your church's worship service.

There will be times and situations where people need encouragement from your wisdom and it will come at an opportune time in their lives. Soul winners need to understand that people need to be encouraged by what they know! Soul winners should see themselves on the front lines in God's army sharing all the spiritual wisdom they have accumulated from the sermons your church provides. What helps the mission of saving souls is when soul winners CONSTANTLY TALK ABOUT WHAT THEY LEARN!

Sharing Baptism Testimonies

One of the most powerful ministries God blessed me to develop during the Coronavirus pandemic was recording the baptism testimonies of Christians. A baptism testimony is simply a two or three-minute personal video recording of a Christian testifying about their conversion process of becoming a baptized believer into Christ. The goal of the baptism testimonies was to articulate how Jesus Christ called each person into the Kingdom of God through the same salvation process of water baptism. (Acts 2:38; 1 Peter 3:20-21; Mark 16:15-16) The baptism testimonies were extremely convincing because people were able to testify about how the gospel message convicted them to come to Jesus and surrender obedience to His gospel despite their struggles.

Lastly, the baptism testimonies afforded soul winners opportunities to get involved through social media. Below are five positive factors that conducting baptism testimonial videos will contribute to the soul-winning efforts of an evangelistic mission.

- The member giving the baptism testimony is involved and reminded of the power, importance, and need to share their salvation experience with the lost.

- The audio/visual media team is involved in working together to make the baptism testimony videos visually attractive.

- The video can be posted on all your social media outlets such as Facebook and YouTube for people to be influenced to become baptized believers.

- The baptism video has the power to encourage sinners to give their lives to Christ once they hear the baptism testimony of other Christian converts.

- Viewing the baptism testimonies will encourage other members to share their own baptism testimony videos.

The art of soul-winning must originate from a sincere love for the souls of humanity in the hopes that God will yield fruit from our efforts. Sharing the word of God is invaluable and incalculable when the seed is planted in good soil. We hope that this chapter has been a blessing in encouraging you to share the message of truth to win souls for Jesus Christ. These methods have been proven to have an enormous impact on the art of soul winning as the Lord has blessed me to see the results of souls being saved. It is my prayer that you will find the same value and effectiveness in these strategies as I have in the effort to win the souls of the lost!

CHAPTER 4

STRATEGY #4: CONDUCT ONE-ON-ONE BIBLE STUDIES

Imagine having Kool-Aid with no sugar, or cereal with no milk. Imagine having Thanksgiving with no turkey! Imagine trying to have sweet potato pie with no sweet potatoes! As incredibly unimaginable as it is to fathom enjoying this food and drink without key ingredients, it is equally unimaginable to conduct evangelism without one-on-one Bible studies. The most powerful ingredient in producing a desirable taste in the soul winning gumbo is the personal Bible study. The absence of the one-on-one

> *The most powerful ingredient in producing a desirable taste in the soul winning gumbo is the personal Bible study.*

Bible study in the soul winning process could be one of the main reasons why churches fail to grow, ministries aren't successful, and evil exists on the level it does now.

Contemplate being filled with honest, truth-seeking questions about God and His word but feeling constantly discouraged over the lack of answers. Questions have kept many people up at night. The lack of quality information and clarity has discouraged many people from believing in God. Unanswered questions have mentally and spiritually positioned many sinners desirous of truth in a place of doubt, disparity, and disdain. However, most of us enjoy the luxury of having someone in our family or friend circles whose non-judgmental demeanor made us feel comfortable enough to confide in them with spiritual questions. Those ministers, confidants, and teachers answered the private personal questions you were embarrassed to ask anyone else for fear they would judge your intelligence and question your integrity.

The Personal One-On-One Bible Study

It is a life-changing experience for truth seekers who are skeptics, agnostics, and even atheists to have answers to questions that have hindered their spiritual progress, stunted their growth, and pounded their hearts with pain. In this chapter of the *Art of Soul Winning* we will discuss in detail a lost art of soul winning that God desires for us to resurrect to save lost souls. I've successfully used the personal Bible study method throughout the years and God has yielded much success in my evangelistic efforts to win souls for Christ. Even in the social media age, by a long shot, this method is still the most effective way to reach lost souls for Jesus Christ. This methodology of converting sinners to Christ is a MUST for those who have secured a seat aboard the Lord's soul train.

In the technology and social media age, we have the blessed privilege of communicating the gospel of Jesus Christ in a multiplicity of ways using the personal one-on-one Bible study method. The one-on-one Bible study method of winning souls can be communicated to sinners through the face-to-face method, virtual methods, social media methods, television method, phone methods, and written Bible correspondence methods through email or regular US postal service mail.

Face-to-Face Bible Studies

The face-to-face method expands far beyond the physical congregational setting and right into someone's kitchen table, couch or coffee shop. The personal Bible study method requires two distinct individuals, a biblically astute teacher and a student(s). The one-on-one personal Bible study method of converting souls to Christ gives students access and the opportunity to ask the teacher questions. The luxury of having scripture properly explained to students can powerfully propel them to understand the word of God.

The face-to-face Bible study method with teacher and student is an intimate, goal-oriented expression of soul concern and love. The face-to-face study method has a profound objective. The objective of this method is to insert God's word of salvation into the heart of a sinner who is lost. Many times sinners are unaware of their status of being lost in the eyes of God. Therefore, some do not understand their need for the gospel of Jesus Christ. I have converted many sinners through the methodology of personal Bible studies who originally believed in their self-manufactured plan and process of accepting Jesus Christ.

Some of those individuals were under the assumption that since they viewed themselves as "good people", God would pardon them for their sins for simply being a so-called "good person" in their own eyes. It was life-changing for most of them to realize that God commanded sinners to obey His salvation process found in scripture for the atonement of their sins. Yes, people are shocked when they come to

> *Yes, people are shocked when they come to understand that the sinner CANNOT create their own individualized personal version of salvation for God to accept.*

understand that the sinner CANNOT create their own individualized personal version of salvation for God to accept. Therefore, the process of being saved by God must originate from God and be authorized by God's word found in the biblical text of scripture.

What's powerful about the personal Bible study phenomenon is the comradery, confidence, conviction, communion, and connection developed between the student and teacher. God produces a kind of evangelistic intimacy between the student and teacher using the word of God like a magnet of spiritual attraction that draws both parties closer to God and each other. Through this personal face-to-face Bible study, the student begins to understand life differently through God's eyes. They begin to see their lives through the lens of God's sovereign power.

Biblical understanding unfolds in a way that would have never taken place outside of the intimate face-to-face setting of a teacher and sinner privately studying God's word. There is a kind of spiritual synergy that develops in one-on-one Bible studies between students and teachers where God releases the sinner's mind from the demonic bondage that has held them in spiritual captivity for years. God redirects the hearts of sinners from a worldly mindset to a Godly mindset. (2 Corinthians 5:14-21) The knowledge of God's grace, mercy, peace, truth and love for them through Jesus Christ is discovered during the personal one-on-one Bible class.

The Goal of Personal Bible Studies

Bible studies with students can have an enormous impact on their souls if the studies are conducted with a goal in mind. If there is no clear, understood objective, the Bible study could easily end up being disappointing to both teacher and student. One-on-one Bible studies take time, energy, effort, patience, and strategic planning. As the facilitator, the soul winner sets the tone and the pace for how the Bible study is conducted.

When the teacher has a desire to accomplish a goal with each study, the student's biblical knowledge will consistently increase. The goal of studying the Bible with a student is to plant the seed of the word of God into the heart of hearers to save their souls through faith, repentance, and baptism into Christ for the forgiveness of sin. (Acts 2:38; 1 Peter 1:22-23)

Conducting Personal Bible Studies

There are rules to conducting Bible studies that must be adhered to if the Bible study interaction is going to be successful. It's important to have a time and date for the Bible study as well as an agreed-upon place to meet. It also helps if the teacher is somewhat familiar with the religious background of the student. This is important because a teacher can develop a plan to use information that is suitable and congruent to the student's spiritual acumen during the Bible study.

Time

When you conduct a one-on-one Bible study it is important to limit the duration of time for the study. You never want to overwhelm the student. I have typically asked and agreed upon a set time of 35 to 40 minutes when studying with a student. A good rule of thumb is to monitor the student's level of engagement while keeping a consistent time for studying. This allows your student to make personal plans after your Bible study without fear that the Bible study will consistently exceed the agreed-upon time.

The face-to-face Bible study method is the only method of personal Bible study where the student and teacher are physically able to see the facial expressions of one another in person. This is helpful when the student is confused since the teacher will notice it in their expression and be able to help even if the student doesn't mention their confusion. As you get more familiar with your student you will quickly learn when they are confused, frustrated, happy, excited or if they are grasping the information in the face-to-face setting.

The Bible Study Setting

The setting is the most underrated and underestimated area of importance in having an engaged Bible study with a student. I learned this the hard way! I can recant and recall entering into a student's home many times and being met with the television blasting, kids running around and dinner being cooked. And during the study, students would answer their cell phone. I quickly realized when I began to study the Bible with students that the setting and surroundings would dictate and determine my student's concentration and engagement. If the Bible study area is a war zone, students become a distracted causality of Bible study warfare, unable to spiritually focus because of the chaotic surroundings. Your teaching can win the soul, but the surrounding of the Bible study can distract the soul, causing the soul to remain lost.

A best practice is to engage the student in a comfortable setting such as a home, coffee shop, restaurant, or church setting where the people and surroundings aren't a distraction. Distractions are detrimental to discipleship. Soul winners must be mindful that their comfort as teachers is equally as important as the student's comfort. If the teacher is distracted by the surroundings, the student will likely be distracted also. The setting of the Bible study can interfere with the goal of the study. The inability to focus because of a chaotic setting can adversely affect the student's attention and engagement and cause them to not be as serious as they should be. Soul winners are wise to strategically manage the dynamics of the environment surrounding the study. Avoiding scenarios that may cause any domestic issues within a student's personal, professional, and family dynamics is strongly recommended.

Scheduling a Personal Bible Study

Soul winners have a multiplicity of approaches at their disposal to initiate conversations with the lost to schedule Bible studies with them. Below are two simple approaches to having conversations with potential students. Both approaches can open the door for scheduling one-on-one personal Bible studies in hopes of converting the lost to Christ.

Indirect Approach | This approach occurs when the objective is not directly communicated, but the conversation is driven towards the objective of discussing Christ in an indirect, conversational manner. (Acts 16:13-15)

Many Christians desire to study the Bible with non-Christians to help them discover Jesus and help them become biblical and scriptural born-again Christians. However, many of those Christians with good intentions do not know how to schedule a personal one-on-one Bible class with those potential students. For over a decade I have scheduled hundreds of personal Bible studies to convert sinners to Christ. Below are a few of the indirect approaches God has blessed me to successfully use to schedule personal Bible studies with new students.

Indirect Approaches to Scheduling Personal Bible Studies

Casual Approach | The indirect approach casually allows the soul winner to plant the seed of studying the Bible without pressing them.

Example: "Part of my daily spiritual routine is studying the Bible. It has helped me tremendously; you should join me sometime in studying once a week for about 30 minutes."

Informative Approach | This indirect approach allows the soul winner to impart the information they have learned and express their passionate desire to share it with loved ones.

Example: "I'm so excited about how much I'm learning from my church's weekly sermons and weekly Bible studies. I would love to share some of these nuggets with you. What day and time are you free during the week to sit down with me for about 30 minutes so I can share what I've learned with you?"

Helpful Approach | This indirect approach allows the soul winner to use the personal Bible study as a helpful tool to aid a potential student. After listening to a potential student's dilemma, this approach is woven into a conversation to provide help for the potential student.

Example: "I've been through a lot myself and I know what you are going through. What helped me get through many situations was the word of God. I would love to sit down with you and go over some of the scriptures that helped me overcome my dilemmas. What day and time will you be free so I can share these biblical gems?"

Needs-Based Approach | This indirect approach allows the soul winners to offer a personal Bible based study on an expressed need mentioned by a potential student in conversation.

Example: "In my devotional Bible study I've read how God's word directly addresses and offers helpful insight on exactly what you've expressed that you need. I'd love to sit down and show you how the word of God can provide direction for you to obtain your needs. When can we sit down and discuss it?

Direct Approaches to Scheduling Personal Bible Studies

Direct Approach | This approach occurs when the objective of discussing the salvation that Jesus Christ provides is more directly communicated in the conversation. This approach typically leads to a response concerning the articulated objective. (Acts 19:1-5) Below are a few of the direct approaches God has blessed me with to successfully use in scheduling personal Bible studies with new students.

Question/Response Approach | Soul winners use this direct methodology in a conversation to raise a spiritual question to a potential student. The goal is to get a response that would prompt the need for a personal one-on-one Bible study to teach the student the gospel of Jesus Christ.

Example: "He said to them, **"Did you receive the Holy Spirit when you believed?"** And they said to him, "No, we have not even heard whether there is a Holy Spirit. 3 And he said, **"Into what then were you baptized?"** And they said, "Into John's baptism." (Acts 19:2-3) In the Question/Response approach spiritual questions are presented in a direct, but non-disrespectful manner to obtain clarity on what and where a believer stands spiritually with their theological beliefs.

Academic Approach | This approach is used by soul winners who desire to take the student to an accurate and deeper level of Bible study.

The Academic approach uses a hermeneutical and exegetical approach to accurately discern scripture for interested students.

Example: "So many times passages of scripture concerning salvation are misinterpreted and honest, unassuming people are given inaccurate information about salvation. Everyone needs to see the truth in the word of God themselves. When can we sit down to study what the word of God actually teaches about salvation?"

Concern Approach | This approach offers soul winners the opportunity to directly approach a student in conversation about their soul when concern for their soul arises in the teacher's heart.

Example: "I really think the world of you and care about where you spend eternity. Will you sit down with me and allow me to show you in God's word what God says a person must do to be saved from sin?"

Correction Approach | This direct approach is used by soul winners to schedule Bible studies with willing students after hearing a student mention they embraced an unbiblical belief concerning their salvation.

Example: "You mentioned something concerning your beliefs about salvation that concerns me. I want to show you what the word of God says so that you can have an accurate understanding of what God requires for sinners to be saved. You can't afford to not know what the Bible says concerning your soul. When can I sit down with you to show you this information?"

You mentioned something concerning your beliefs about salvation that concerns me.

Relevant Life Approach | The soul winner uses this approach based on observing the student's life. The teacher asks for a personal Bible study to show the person in need how God's word provides help for their current life issue without the student asking for help.

Example: "There is something in God's word that I need to show you that will bless your life tremendously! Let's sit down together and have a Bible study to discuss how God's word can help you. I want us to pray together as well. When can we sit down to study and pray?"

The indirect and direct approaches for scheduling personal one on one Bible studies are for every Christian to engage in. These strategies are not only effective in initiating the conversation, they can also get people to the kitchen table. The kitchen table isn't reduced to the consumption of physical food. The kitchen table is also for the consumption of spiritual food when teacher and student study God's word together. Personalities often dictate what method or approach is best, but use wisdom, passion, and aggressiveness to schedule your personal Bible studies so that God uses you to save the lost!

Closing the Deal

There are many teaching techniques, methods, and ways that aid students to discover the urgency of saying **yes** to a relationship with Jesus Christ during a Bible study. A teacher's primary job is to give their students enough understandable biblical evidence to obey the gospel of Jesus Christ through faith, repentance, and baptism. (Acts 2:36-41) After conducting hundreds of Bible studies, I have concluded that teachers must learn how to **close to deal** when teaching personal Bible studies. Just as an experienced salesman knows how to close the sale, an experienced soul winner must know how to close the soul. Although teachers should not make decisions for their students, they must know how to close the deal to secure the soul.

After sharing God's plan of salvation with numerous students, I've discovered many students won't give any indication of their need to apply what you've shared with them in the Bible study. This leaves much ambiguity between both the teacher and the student once the study is completed. A Bible study best practice is to ask your student some **application questions**. An **application question** is a question strategically designed to arouse your student's thinking toward applying what they have read and what they understand from God's word.

> *A Bible study best practice is to ask your student some application questions.*

Below are a few **application questions** that soul winners should ask students before the conclusion of each Bible study. Application questions should be presented in love to bring light to the urgency of deciding on God's instructions for sinners to be saved.

- What questions do you have about today's Bible lesson?

- What stood out to you about today's Bible lesson?

- Is there anything you read that wasn't clear that I can help you understand better?

- What do you think you should **do** about what you learned today?

- Do you think you need to repent and be baptized for the remission of your sins?

- Based on what you have read, do you believe God wants you to repent of your sins and be baptized for the remission of your sins?

- If a student says "yes" to the aforementioned question of their need to repent and be baptized, the next application question is **when would you like to do that?**

- If a student indicates their desire to be baptized **immediately,** be prepared to have someone readily available to baptize them the same day.

- If a student says they desire to be baptized on a future date, it's fine for them to do so. However, every student needs the option of being baptized immediately. It's not ever wise to push anyone to be baptized the same day unless the student sees the urgent need to do so. Also, have the student read Acts 2:41 and point out that the first initial converts of Christianity were baptized the same day after they gladly received the word. By reading the passage of Acts 2:41 it may encourage your student to respond immediately to the urgency of baptism for the forgiveness of their sins. (Acts 2:38)

- Are you comfortable in your current state of being unforgiven of sin?

- Are you comfortable knowing Jesus Christ could return at any time to **repay** eternal punishment to those who didn't faithfully respond to His sacrificial death with obedience?

- Are you comfortable knowing Jesus Christ could return at any time to **reward** those in His church who faithfully obeyed Him with eternal pleasure?

- If the student indicates their discomfort concerning their state as a sinner, ask the next application questions. **What does God**

require you to do based on the scriptures you've read? After the student articulates God's biblical requirements ask, **when would you like to do what God requires?**

- Is there anything in your mind that is causing any hesitancy about obeying the truth of God's gospel? If so, ask the student to tell you their hesitancy so you can help.

These are just a few of the application questions that have been extremely useful to me in **closing the soul** and baptizing sinners into Christ for the forgiveness of their sins. I trust these application questions will be useful to anyone willing to use them to convert the lost to Christ.

Virtual Evangelism

It happened on a Thursday afternoon during the global Coronavirus pandemic. I got a call at the office. A sister in Christ contacted my office and said her friend was desirous of giving his life to Jesus Christ and wanted to be baptized for the forgiveness of his sins. Naturally, I was excited for him and began thinking about setting a time for this gentleman to meet me at our church building in Louisville, Kentucky to baptize him.

Then the sister told me that her friend lived in a state 800 miles away (an eleven-hour drive). She told me this gentleman had been watching our ministries' videos on Facebook live and decided to give his life to Jesus. I quickly contacted a local gospel preacher in the city and state the brother lived in to help him be baptized. The local preacher contacted the gentleman and the brother was baptized into Christ the same day.

On another occasion during the transmission of this book I received a message on our church Facebook page from a woman who was searching for a church home. After reaching out and praying with her, I discovered she was spiritual, honest and sincere, but needed some biblical teaching to aid in her understanding. She agreed to study the Bible on the Zoom platform. Zoom is a virtual platform that gives participants opportunities to see each other's faces virtually while they converse. Though we were not in the same room, this virtual platform gave us a powerful way to communicate without having any physical interaction. The next week she decided to be baptized into Jesus Christ for the remission of sins after our second virtual Bible study.

The Missing Link

Most of the popular virtual platforms such as Facebook, YouTube, and Zoom all have sharable links for their videos. A video link from these platforms can simply be copied and pasted to send to people via text, messenger, or email to willing hearers. If one video link of a presentation of the gospel is shared it can be the missing link between a sinner and Jesus Christ. The power of the gospel of Jesus Christ is God's love to save humanity from sin, despair, desperation, guilt, shame, and eternal condemnation. Soul winners must familiarize themselves with the art of presenting the gospel message of Jesus Christ through the avenue of social media by sharing a link from a virtual platform. This method can save souls! I am a witness to seeing this soul-winning phenomenon come to fruition for the glory of God!

Power Link

There will always be soul winners who want to spread the gospel but cannot teach the gospel. This is the kind of soul winner who uses their spiritual influence to connect the lost with trusted ministry leaders. These soul winners know how to use creative ways to get people to the waters of baptism but may not be comfortable teaching them to get there. Some teach, but others just know how to bring the lost to a teacher.

In a very real sense, sharing a video link to spread that gospel could be a powerful method of evangelism for determined soul winners. Yes, if presented in a quality manner, one shared link could be a powerful link between Jesus and a sinner! Soul winners come in all different forms and with a multiplicity of abilities. Becoming effective to reach the lost should be the goal for each soul winner. Using the power link method of sharing virtual videos can be very effective in saving the lost for those who aggressively promote Christ through this approach.

Virtual Evangelism Videos

I typically use a six-lesson series to convert the lost to Christ. I also teach my soul-winning teams how to convert souls to Christ using the same methodology. However, some soul winners aren't always comfortable teaching, but there are ways for them to get the necessary teaching to their students. Virtual evangelism is an effective method to use. Here's how it works. I have six pre-recorded videos teaching each one of the six paper lessons I use to convert the lost to Christ. Each video is about twenty-five minutes.

Through the pre-recorded virtual evangelism videos, all soul winners have to do is send the link of the video for their students to watch along with each paper lesson. After the student watches the video and completes each paper lesson, they simply submit it to the soul winner who sent them the power link. This works. I've seen people converted to Christ and be baptized into Christ using the Virtual Evangelism video method. I've discovered that if people can purchase workout videos and follow the instructions to get their desired results, we can do the same in the Church with evangelism to get the results that Christ died for!

By using the six lessons Virtual Evangelism series, soul winning teams just need to know how to send the attached link with a lesson. Then the soul winner must follow up with the student to review the student's lesson as well as answer their questions. The link you send a student could not only be their missing link to Christ, but also their power link to receive the power of God unto salvation. (Romans 1:16-17) As a ministry leader, teaching this method to my soul winning team allows me to be in multiple places teaching without needing to be physically there. Also, I can remove any teaching burden from my soul winners when they are not comfortable with certain individuals or feel they cannot teach them.

Lastly, there are many social media platforms available for persons to hear biblical information about Jesus to be saved. The one-on-one Bible study method between teacher and student can be very effective in converting the sinner. The challenge becomes utilizing the most effective one-on-one method to obtain the results you desire. Face-to-face Bible studies and evangelistic virtual videos are all viable methods I've witnessed that have provided a vast amount of soul winning victories. Today, soul winners have a powerful advantage to engage people for Jesus, more so than in times past. Utilize the best personal Bible study method that your student feels comfortable with to communicate the gospel of Jesus Christ.

Visitor Cards

A while back we were waiting on a package of significance to arrive in the mail at the church building. This package wasn't sent via certified mail, so we had no way of tracking it. Weeks went by and the package never showed up. Finally, my secretary went to the Post Office and lo and behold it was there! The package was being held at the Post Office because of some mailing issue, but I never thought to look for the package at the Post Office. That experience made me realize that many times the things we desire are right under our nose. If we fail to look for them, we can miss out on what's already there. Evangelism is the same way. Lost souls can be hiding in plain sight!

Lost souls can be hiding in plain sight!

Most ministries have implemented some method to collect visitor information from those who physically visit their church assemblies. If your ministry is still old school and has yet to implement an electronic method to do this, the good news is that the paper method of collecting visitor information still works! The cards used to gather visitor's information are universally referred to as visitor cards.

The reality of visitor cards is that they consist of people who have entered your building and already been in your midst. These people all have needs and have provided your ministry with the information to contact them! I strongly believe that if a ministry has a strategy to aggressively approach the visitors, there is an entirely new Church in your visitor cards! Yes, a completely different group of people who have already come to your assembly have given you access to contact them. Visitor cards provide opportunities to save lost souls.

Below is a method of contacting people who left visitor cards that could aid your soul winning ministry tremendously. Members of your soul winning team simply need to gather the visitor cards and contact the visitors utilizing the script below. The goal is to portray you and your ministry as friendly in hopes that your sincere efforts will allow you to minister to individuals who have visited your church.

Visitor Card Call Script

Good evening! My name is _____ from the _____ **Church of Christ**. I'm calling on behalf of our minister, _____ how are you? You visited our church on_____ and I wanted to personally thank you for visiting. We wanted to follow up with you to let you know we are still thinking of you. Do you have any **prayer requests** or **spiritual needs** that I can help you with by praying with you right now?

If yes, gather what's in their hearts and pray for them on the spot, then proceed to the church invitation.

If no, proceed to the church invitation below.

Our Life-Changing Worship Service starts EACH SUNDAY at _____ and we would love to worship God with you again in hopes that you would benefit from the Word of God and the fellowship. We also meet each week for Bible study at _____. Would you need transportation to worship with us? **If yes**, confirm their address and advise them you will have someone from the Transportation Ministry contact them.

If no, proceed to encouragement information below.

Encouragement: We have several ministries designed to meet the needs of our members and our community. Please let us know if you have any Bible questions concerning salvation or questions on improving the quality of your life. We can schedule a personal Bible class to give you Bible answers for your Bible questions.

End call: I've enjoyed talking to you. God bless you and we look forward to seeing you soon at the _____ **Church of Christ!**

****Make all weekly calls no later than Wednesday and
do not call past 8 pm.****

CHAPTER 5

TEACH THE TEACHER TO TEACH

There are some extremely effective soul-winning teaching strategies and principles that every evangelism team utilizing the one-on-one teaching method should find useful. These effective strategies in The Art of Soul Winning can save souls, transform lives, grow sustainable churches, engage communities and change the trajectory of a family's generational spirituality forever.

There is nothing more fulfilling than having a burning desire to reach the lost by showing them the love and process of salvation that Jesus's sacrificial death provides. What every ministry needs is a team of dedicated individuals with a sincere desire to win souls. Next, we will teach the teacher how to teach. It's the teaching that will aid in your evangelistic efforts to place sinners in contact and communication with the cleansing blood of Jesus Christ.

Desire

"The fruit of the righteous is a tree of life, and he that winneth souls is wise."
– Proverbs 11:30 KJV

There is an **"art"** to winning souls. **Art** is that which derives from the creative genius of a skillful artist when it's put on display. Disciples have to discover and develop the art of soul winning. Do you have a desire to win souls? Are you motivated to win souls? Motivation and desire are inextricably linked. Therefore, becoming motivated to win souls for Jesus Christ comes from several belief factors which create desire.

> *There is an "**art**" to winning souls.*

- Your **worldview** is a contributing factor in having a **desire** to win souls. (John 1:1; Genesis 1:1)

- Your view of **humanity** is a contributing factor in having a **desire** to win souls. (Romans 3:23; John 8:21-24; 2 Thessalonians 1:6-12)

- Your **firm belief in God and His Word** is a contributing factor in having a **desire** to win souls. (John 4:42; 16:27-30; 2 Timothy 2:1-2)

- Your view of **Messianic authority** is a contributing factor in having a **desire** to win souls. (Mark 16:15; Matthew 28:16-20)

- Your view of **God's reward system** is a contributing factor in having a **desire** to win souls. (Proverbs 11:30; Matthew 19:27-30)

A functional and spiritual view of the factors that contribute to "soul winning" will help you gain the confidence needed to develop the art of having soul-saving conversations. Do you KNOW someone that is LOST without an AUTHENTIC RELATIONSHIP with Jesus supported by biblical Truth?

SOUL WINNING ASSIGNMENT: Allow your desire to save souls motivate you to have a conversation with someone each day with a personal goal of scheduling a personal one-on-one Bible study.

Indoctrination through Observation

Evangelism is the process of proclaiming the good news of Jesus Christ's atonement for our sins. This good news of the gospel occurs in the process of soul winning when a **desire** to save souls and an **opportunity** to save souls kiss each other. However, opportunities to spread the gospel may not always be plentiful. Soul winners should constantly seek opportunities to share the word of God. The Lord uses very random occasions for believers to bring souls to Jesus Christ. Nonetheless, one of the most impactful practices in the art of teaching personal Bible studies is observing the teaching needs of a student.

**Notice some factors that soul winners may
OBSERVE in a potential student.**

"Now a Jew named Apollos, an Alexandrian by birth, an eloquent man, came to Ephesus; and he was mighty in the Scriptures. 25 This man had been instructed in the way of the Lord; and being fervent in spirit, he was speaking and teaching accurately the things concerning Jesus, being acquainted only with the baptism of John; 26 and he began to speak out boldly in the synagogue. But when Priscilla and Aquila heard him, they took him aside and explained to him the way of God more accurately."
– Acts 18:24-26

- Students may be of various ethnic, racial, and geographical backgrounds.

- Students may be eloquent (gifted with learning).

- Students may be powerful in their knowledge of scripture.

- Students may be instructed in God's way.

- Students may be fervent in spirit.

- Students may be presently teaching some accurate teachings concerning Christ.

- Students may be limited in the knowledge of critical areas of understanding concerning the will of our Lord and Savior, Jesus Christ.

- Students may be unaware of the fullness of Christ's teaching.

- Students may have already been baptized before. (Act 19:1-5)

- Students may already be worshippers of God. (Acts 16:14-15)

Notice some factors that will AID in scheduling personal Bible studies.

"Now a Jew named Apollos, an Alexandrian by birth, an eloquent man, came to Ephesus; and he was mighty in the Scriptures. 25 This man had been instructed in the way of the Lord; and being fervent in spirit, he was speaking and teaching accurately the things concerning Jesus, being acquainted only with the baptism of John; 26 and he began to speak out boldly in the synagogue. But when Priscilla and Aquila heard him, they took him aside and explained to him the way of God more accurately."
– Acts 18:24-26

- Teachers must be active listeners, urgently prepared to respond to teaching errors.

- Teachers must be methodical in choosing the appropriate methods to respond to the error.

- Teachers must be able to pull willing hearers aside in non-hostile settings to teach them.

- Teachers must be able to explain the truth accurately.

Understanding Scripture

A scriptural understanding is a bridge to a strong spiritual relationship with God. Individuals with an understanding of scripture can experience the joy, freedom, grace, salvation, forgiveness, love, and hope found in Christ Jesus. Teachers of the gospel need to be informed of some basic realities concerning student and teacher interaction to conduct effective Bible studies.

In Acts 8:31-32, we find an encounter in the word of God between a saved man and a sinner. This interaction took place in an intimate learning atmosphere which fostered a powerful and critical explanation of the word of God. The criticality of this seemingly random Bible study was the fact that it aided a sinner's understanding of scripture so that salvific truth could be realized. The biblical interaction between student and teacher in Acts 8:31-32 demonstrates God's ability to connect truth-seekers with truth teachers.

"Philip ran up and heard him reading Isaiah the prophet, and said, 'Do you understand what you are reading?' And he said, 'Well, how could I unless someone guides me?' And he invited Philip to come up and sit with him.'"

– Acts 8:31-32

Notice some OBSERVATIONS from these verses of scripture.

- People read scripture.

- People who read scripture do not always understand scripture.

- People who read scripture do not believe that they can understand scripture without a teacher to guide them.

- People who read scripture need a teacher to guide them.

- People who read scripture need a teacher to guide them into an accurate understanding.

- People who read scripture must humble themselves to invite a teacher to guide them into accurate understanding.

- People who read scripture who humble themselves to invite a teacher to guide them need a teacher who will run to help them.

- People who read scripture need a teacher who will ask them if they understand what they read.

- People who read scripture need patient teachers.

- People who read scripture may already be worshippers of God.

A functional and spiritual view of the factors that contribute to soul winning will help you gain the confidence needed to develop the art of having soul-saving conversations. Do you KNOW someone who is LOST without an AUTHENTIC RELATIONSHIP with Jesus supported by biblical Truth?

SOUL WINNING ASSIGNMENT: Using the strategies we've discussed thus far, <u>list 12 people</u> that you could have a conversation with to <u>schedule a personal one-on-one Bible study to teach them gospel truth</u>. After using your preferred approach, be mindful to confirm a date, time, location, or social media platform to study with your student for no more than 30 to 45 minutes.

_____   _____

_____   _____

_____   _____

_____   _____

_____   _____

_____   _____

The Mechanics of Distributing Knowledge

Have you ever had the experience of hearing information communicated in a way that turned your interest away from the topic of conversation more so than attracting you to it? The mechanics of how information is communicated to people hearing is important for them to effectively grasp the information. There are some teaching mechanics in the treatment of "knowledge" that helps people hearing understand

and obey the gospel of Jesus Christ. Let's explore the mechanics of knowledge by dissecting the first gospel sermon after the resurrection of Jesus Christ. The goal of a soul winner is to effectively get **knowledge** into a sinner's head and heart so that they receive the help they need.

KNOWLEDGE must intellectually get into a sinner's HEAD

*"Therefore let all the house of Israel **know** for certain that God has made Him both Lord and Christ—this Jesus whom you crucified."*
– Acts 2:36

The word "know" in Acts 2:36 is an original Greek word ginóskó (γινώσκω) that means "to take in knowledge or come to a realization". In the mechanics of knowledge, the audience of Peter's preaching was instructed to "**know**" for certain that God had made Jesus both Lord and Christ. (Acts 2:36) It's paramount for a student to understand Jesus in the way God intended for Christ to be understood. For humanity to appreciate His coming, death by crucifixion and His resurrection as both Lord and Christ, the specifics of that in-depth knowledge have to be emphasized by a teacher.

Sinners become convicted when they come to the **knowledge** that God made our crucified Jesus, both Lord, and Christ. Without learning the accuracy of this knowledge, there is no salvific certainty of one's salvation.

KNOWLEDGE must emotionally get into a sinner's HEART

*"Now when they **heard this**, they were pierced to the **heart**, and said to Peter and the rest of the apostles, "Brethren, what shall we do?"*
— Acts 2:37

99

After hearing and receiving the knowledge of the crucified Christ, the men of Israel's hearts were pierced. (Acts 2:37) The word pierced means "to violently prick". The intellectual knowledge of Jesus led these sinners to feel emotionally overwhelmed to respond favorably to His sacrifice. The knowledge of the gospel pierced these sinner's hearts after hearing the sacrifice of Christ. The guilt of their sins impacted these sinner's hearts emotionally.

KNOWLEDGE must responsively move a sinner to seek HELP

*"Now when they **heard this**, they were pierced to the **heart**, and said to Peter and the rest of the apostles, "**Brethren, what shall we do?**"*
– Acts 2:37

After the knowledge of the crucified Christ entered into the heads and hearts of sinners, they sought help. These sinners responded by seeking help when they asked the question, "Brethren, what shall we do?" (Acts 2:37) The knowledge of the gospel moved them to respond to **DO SOMETHING** to release their guilt.

*"Peter said to them, "**Repent**, and each of you **be baptized in the name of Jesus Christ for the forgiveness of your sins**; and you will receive the gift of the Holy Spirit."*
– Acts 2:38

After believing in Jesus, Peter gave instructions to the sinners who desperately needed freedom from the guilt of their sins. Filled with the Holy Spirit, Peter told them to repent and be baptized in the name of Jesus Christ for the forgiveness of their sins. (Acts 2:38) Receiving the knowledge of God's plan of salvation from Peter provided the spiritual direction they needed to relieve their guilt of sin through faithful obedience to God's instructions. (Acts 2:38; 41)

> *"So then, those who had received his word were baptized; and that day there were added about three thousand souls."*
> **– Acts 2:41**

In one sermon roughly three thousand guilty souls were forgiven of the sins they committed because they responded faithfully to the knowledge they received. (Acts 2:41) Lacking the knowledge of how God intended for sinners to be forgiven has caused much religious confusion, inadequate beliefs, and teachings that have distorted the understanding of honest people for thousands of years. The mechanics of distributing God's knowledge for the salvation of mankind to be forgiven of sin will make a world of difference. Individuals can be confident in knowing they are saved when the knowledge of God's will for salvation has been scripturally discovered, understood, and adhered to.

The factors that contribute to soul winning will help you gain the confidence needed to develop the art of having soul-saving conversations. Review the teaching strategies in this chapter and use one of the approaches mentioned in your discussions with potential students to schedule a personal Bible study. Your effort could lead someone to the pardoning of their sins through a relationship with Jesus Christ.

STUDY GUIDE

Baptism is a widely debated and argued spiritual practice among religious circles. Nevertheless, according to Jesus Christ water baptism is necessary for a sinner to receive the forgiveness of their sins, the gift of the Holy Spirit, and entrance to the Lord's church. (Mark 16:15-16; Acts 2:36-47) To baptize people in the social media age, people must be taught and exposed to the gospel of Jesus Christ. Soul winners should remain busy putting sinners in the watery grave and the liquid tomb of baptism! Below are ten BAPTISM BEST PRACTICES to help convert sinners to Christ through the faith response of baptism.

Baptism Best Practices

- **Salvation story** | Before you engage in a personal bible study ask your student to share their personal salvation story in detail. Allow them to articulate the process of how they became saved. Document your student's experience for proof of their understanding of salvation. This will give you evidence of the process of their salvation in their own words. The beauty of this is if your students' understanding of salvation is different from what God has commanded in scripture, you have a platform to show them the truth and evidence of their error. Trust God to open the hearts of your students to respond to the gospel of Jesus Christ. (Acts 16:14-15)

- **The blood in baptism** | Baptism saves. (1 Peter 3:21) God saves us through the faith act of baptism. (Acts 2:36-47; 1 Peter 3:21) It's not the element of water itself that saves us, it's the God who authorizes the teaching of baptism who uses the blood of Jesus as a cleansing agent to save sinners. (Hebrews 9:22; 10:11-4; Colossians 2:13) God saves us when we obey God's command to be baptized in water for the remission of sins. (Matthew 26:28; Acts 2:38)

- **<u>Converted to Christ</u>** | Baptism is the culminating act of obeying the gospel. We tend to overemphasize baptism and under-emphasize the preaching of Jesus, belief, repentance, and confession. Thus, when baptism is overly emphasized, we make the focus on what people can receive instead of the commitment of what they are expected to give God as a child of God once receiving forgiveness of sins. This leads to vampire Christianity. Vampire Christianity occurs when people want to receive the benefits of the blood but want nothing to do with the discipleship that comes with a relationship with Jesus Christ.

- **<u>Teach people Jesus!</u>** | What converts people to Christ is powerful teaching of who Jesus Christ is and what He did. Emphasize Jesus' death, burial, and resurrection. People must know Jesus Christ for themselves, not just what Jesus offers. They need to know Him! Preach Jesus! (Acts 8:35; Philippians 3:15)

- **<u>The One Baptism</u>** | The Bible teaches the concept of the "one baptism" (Ephesians 4:5). Many people have experienced some form of baptism and have been baptized multiple times in multiple ways. Some have been sprinkled and some have been immersed. Your primary responsibility is more than just teaching people the error of their previous baptism. A soul winner's job is to teach the truth about biblical salvation which encompasses water baptism. Honest students will likely desire to be baptized correctly once they read the distinction between biblical baptism versus their personal baptism experiences if their understanding of scripture was in error. Those who refuse to obey Jesus with a more accurate understanding of scripture should be a non-issue to you. You've planted the seed, so be happy and content with that. If your student's baptism appears invalid or illegitimate to you as their teacher, God must bring desire to their hearts to make that correction. The gospel comes to fruition when people develop a heart of submission to Christ. Otherwise, people will become baptized because you pushed them to, without having made a personal conviction to repent and respond to Christ's sacrifice for themselves.

- **Baptism is Essential** | According to Jesus, sinners cannot be saved before they are baptized. (Mark 16:15-16) One can be saved with baptism, but one cannot be saved without it. (1 Peter 3:21) It's an indisputable Christological fact that will not change whether people accept it or not.

- **Baptism was consistently practiced in Scripture** | Baptism was a consistent spiritual practice and process in the New Testament. Sinners were introduced to Jesus Christ through burial in water, a faith response called baptism. At and after the inception of the church, everyone saved in the New Testament was saved by Christ in the same way, through baptism. You have a vast amount of consistent historical baptism accounts in the Bible to prove that. (Acts 2:38-41; Acts 8:35-39; Acts 9:18; Acts 10:47-48)

- **Hearts must be opened by God** | When people are honest, they will obey the gospel of Christ. Being baptized must be a sinner's heart response and decision. (Acts 16:14-15)

- **<u>Emphasize the Savior's Sacrifice</u>** | Emphasize the death, burial, and resurrection of Jesus Christ. (1 Corinthians 15:1-4)

- **<u>Baptism births Christianity</u>** | Baptism is great, but it's just the genesis of a person being born again. When a baby has been birthed they start the process of growing. Likewise, after baptism, Christians must be consistently fed the word of God to grow spiritually. Build strong spiritual relationships with your students that will last a lifetime through your appreciation of our Lord's sacrifice for our sins.

Strategic Soul Winning Discipleship

CHAPTER 6

STRATEGY #5: BE CONSISTENT

How would you feel if you showed up at the hospital for major surgery and the top surgeon you expected to operate on you didn't show up? What if your barber or beautician randomly started missing your weekly scheduled hair appointments? When you have important scheduled events to attend, would you be concerned by the failure of these professionals to appreciate your time, trust, and confidence by not showing up for the appointment you set with them? Imagine finding out that your babysitter leaves your children unattended or has someone less competent attend to your children unbeknownst to you?

We all need consistency in our lives. People pay big money for consistency. When people are satisfied with the consistency they receive, they will typically inform others about how great a specific person, product, procedure, or process was that helped them enjoy their desired results.

We all need consistency in our lives.

People notice patterns of consistency, especially as they relate to something they have become accustomed to enjoying. But people also notice inconsistencies. I've learned that people appreciate consistency, respect it, and expect it. The development of consistency in the soul winning process happens when a consistently scheduled pattern of contact and communication occurs.

To be effective in winning souls, spiritual content should be routinely, regularly, and consistently distributed to those with whom you are in contact. Spiritual contact may consist of personal visits, devotional videos, prayer, sermons, concerts, follow-up phone calls, text messages, and emails. Consistent contact and conducting consistent ministries on a daily, weekly, or monthly basis will increase the chances of connecting someone to Christ.

Consistent Content

In the social media age, there are too many people, places, things, churches, and ministries competing for people's attention. While copious amounts of content might be produced consistently and made widely available in the technological age, not every ministry produces the most accurate biblical teachings. Nor do they operate with biblical integrity. Online and television consumers view many of these ministries as trusted sources of spiritual content because they produce "consistent" content. When spiritual consumers don't know the accuracy of biblical truth they can easily be led astray. This means some people get caught up in the hype of false biblical content without realizing that what they are hearing is not rooted in the Bible. If in-person, online, or television consumers do not know the difference between truth and error, they could digest a demonic diet of destruction.

Soul winners can become a viable, reliable, and trusted biblical source for consumers if they can constantly and consistently produce content relative to biblical truths. They can also be soul winners by helping viewers discern what online biblical content is actually based on Bible truths. Although your ministry may have more accurate biblical content on social media, you can get labeled as "inconsistent" in the minds of many people if you haven't begun producing "consistent" content.

Consistent Follow-Up

People systematically develop their lifestyles around what consistently impacts their life. If hearing the word of God is consistently communicated on their cell phones, social media pages, email, and text messages, at some point they are going to click that link and see what all the fuss is about. Once they click the link from your devotion, sermon, or worship service there must be something that connects them with the truth. The content must encompass something inspiring, engaging, attractive, and relative to their spiritual senses which arrest their attention! However, once people have been exposed to the word of God, unfortunately, many soul winners skip the most important step. They don't follow up with the people they communicate the word of God to.

Soul winning truly becomes art or science when a schedule is consistently applied based on when, where, and how contact is made with those you are seeking to attract to Christ. A follow-up date/time must be included in the follow-up process for attracting the lost.

Prospect list

Saving souls MUST become an intentional act. Salvation is a deliverance from the danger, penalty, and punishment that sinners await. Salvation also serves as an unmerited status of righteousness for those who have chosen a relationship with our Sovereign Sinless Savior Jesus Christ. For those who are devoid of having a faithful relationship with Jesus, the eternal dwelling of their souls will be in

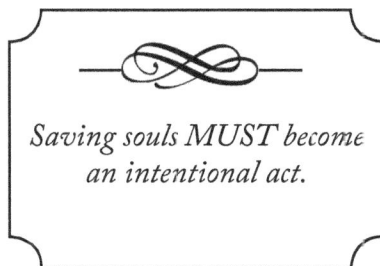

> *Saving souls MUST become an intentional act.*

a place Jesus and the word of God refer to as hell. Hell is the geographic location where the punishment for the unfaithful and disobedient will occur. (Matthew 10:28-31)

Soul winners understand the soul is the truest essence of the human personality and the most authentic version of an individual. The soul is the part of you that understands, possesses the knowledge, believes, feels pain, laughter and joy, cries, hurts, and heals. Essentially, the soul is the core of who you are within the fabric of your human existence. Sadly, everyone who has a soul does not understand the value and eternal destiny of their departed souls in the spiritual realm. Soul winners must help people see the need and necessity to secure their souls in the safety of the blood of Jesus Christ for eternity.

Ready for Random Prospects

"A woman named Lydia, from the city of Thyatira, a seller of purple fabrics, a worshiper of God, was listening; and the Lord opened her heart to respond to the things spoken by Paul. 15 And when she and her household had been baptized, she urged us, saying, "If you have judged me to be faithful to the Lord, come into my house and stay." And she prevailed upon us."
– Acts 16:14-15

One day the Apostle Paul and those accompanying him went searching for a place to pray. Paul ended up having a random conversation with some women down by a riverside. This conversation with the women led to Paul sharing the word of Christ with them. A leading woman named Lydia and her household were baptized into Christ after what appeared to be a random conversation with Paul. Though this interaction appears **random**, God planned the interaction with a purpose. He opened the hearts of those people so they could respond to His word as revealed by the Lord. (Acts 16:14-15) Soul winners must be ready to present the word of God at all times.

This teaches us that you never know when and where God will use you, so always be ready. Wherever a soul winner has human interactions, we MUST understand that every soul we encounter is either going to be won for Christ or lost to the devil. With God, there are no unintentional interactions.

> *Wtih God, there are no unintentional interactions.*

Soul winners are wise to develop a list of persons with whom they have an existing or growing relationship who need to know Jesus. The list of prospects should consist of family members, friends, loved ones, co-workers, and those you have frequent interactions with. Some people would enjoy a personal phone call while others would prefer a text message.

When sending content to potential Christian prospects, what will you send that individual? Will you send them salvation lessons, Bible verses, sermon links from YouTube, or biblical wisdom quotes? Some people may be hesitant to respond to your communication and some will occasionally respond. Others will respond consistently. Ultimately, your prayer is that God opens the hearts of sinners to respond to the truth of God's word once it enters their hearts.

Follow Up Routine

After planting the seed of truth into the hearts of the lost, soul winners need to decide the frequency of their follow-up routine. How often will biblical and spiritual information be communicated? Whether it's daily, weekly, bi-weekly, or once a month, the communication must be consistent. Oftentimes people will disregard powerful spiritual information until life places them in a situation where they need inspiration and encouragement. Your phone call, text, visit, or spiritual post on social media can encourage someone in a way you could never imagine.

I've shared the word of God and someone later articulated to me that God used me to save their life. I don't know what it was that I said or the nature of the situation the person was going through. All I know is that the Lord used me to say something to encourage them and I praise God for it. I've seen people with grave diseases who advised me that God had powerfully used our ministry's virtual platforms to minister to their needs. Sometimes soul winners fail to realize how their consistency in distributing God's word encourages people in hospitals, hospices, and places of despair. The word of God helps get people through arduous situations.

When soul winners consistently follow up with potential students it leads to opportunities for them to get comfortable asking questions about salvation or religious matters that have troubled them. When students ask questions, it's a good sign the recipients of your consistent messaging believe you are creditable, reliable, and integral. The follow-up also gives soul winners a chance to pray for the person in need. Those prayers will provide relief, hope, and blessings in the lives of souls who need to know Jesus Christ. In the follow-up process, I've contacted many people and asked them if I could pray for them. I do not recall anyone ever turning me down for praying for them!

In an era of protests, a pandemic, and political unrest, I've discovered that people need hope, direction, and a reliable spiritual fixture in their lives. People are searching for ministry leaders and workers they can rely on to provide the four essentials in humanity; love, forgiveness, grace, and truth. All four of those essentials are found in the person of Jesus Christ.

Will you make a declaration to consistently communicate and dialogue with the lost? Doing so may help a sinner become susceptible to obeying our Sovereign Savior in the social media age.

CHAPTER 7

STRATEGY #6: CONNECT

"Everyone communicates, but few connect."
– John Maxwell

As an Evangelist during the coronavirus pandemic of 2020 and 2021, I experienced the paradigm of having to shift my entire ministry to virtual platforms for the safety of our congregants. I witnessed, experienced, and lived through the pros and cons of this unprecedented virtual shift. I'm thankful God afforded us creative ministry workers with hearts for Him to carry out His kingdom mission amid much adversity. However, many ministry workers are only concerned with the personal perks they can get from God. I'm glad to have been fortunate enough to be connected with some laborers who only desire ministry for what they can give to God! To give your best kingdom efforts to win the lost in this virtual society, we must develop strategies to **connect** with them. Biblical communicators must connect!

Biblical communicators must connect!

Connection demands efforts from both the listener as well as the communicator. We live in a sound-bite world where people in the 21st century have very short attention spans. Many consumers of spiritual content are only interested in brief amounts of content less than 60 seconds in length. Our current cultural climate loves impressive punchlines and hearing sticky statements sometimes without even knowing the validity or original context of some of the verbal content.

Some only read headlines without reading the entirety of the actual lines in a publication. Split-second Christianity is a thing where your content only has a few seconds to connect with someone in the social media realm. Without an instant connection, many listeners will dismiss what they have heard as something they can't connect with, having not even really listened to it!

For souls to be won for Christ in the social media age, people need to connect with content that's relevant to their lives. Without a relationship with Christ, people do not know how valuable the life of Christ is to humanity. Christ should not be presented in evangelism efforts as an optional figure, but a necessary fixture in the lives of humanity. This means that verbal and video content in ministry must address needs within the human experience. Sin is a part of the human experience. Thus, the biblical content presented in ministry must exist as a necessity for mankind's spiritual diet.

When connecting, communicators must understand their audiences and the anthropological attractions people have toward obtaining a better quality of life. Most God-fearing people want security, hope, forgiveness, grace, improvement, spiritual guidance, and direction. If a ministry is going to attract souls in both physical and virtual assemblies, the content must consist of what connects with people. Humanity yearns for God's response to their human plight. Communicators must simply present God's biblical responses to humanity's inadequacies in an understandable way that can be practically applied.

To be effective, an Evangelist must know how to connect with people. When people are disconnected, they go astray because having a strong connection is important for spiritual stability. In our current technological age, many consumers own high-resolution 4k smart televisions and pay for expensive high-speed internet at their homes to use their electronic devices. Without an internet connection, most of our electronics functionalities become limited or useless.

In like manner, powerful spiritual content is ineffective if it's communicated in ways devoid of connection. For example, some of you reading this may have had the experience of trying to connect your phone, iPad, or laptop to Wi-Fi. Depending on your location and signal strength, you could see a display that says WEAK CONNECTION. This signal appears because the Wi-Fi strength in your current location isn't strong enough. The absence of a strong connection affects the speed at which you can move on the internet and the same is true in ministry. Notice a few areas where a soul winning ministry can effectively connect with sinners.

Salvation

There is no doubt that the ultimate goal for Christians is to persuade the lost to obey the gospel of Jesus Christ. (Mark 16:15-16; Mathew 28:19-20) When this occurs souls are won for God and snatched from the devil. (2 Thessalonians. 1:6-10) The question becomes, what is the best way to connect with people to usher them into a saved relationship with Jesus Christ culminating in the waters of baptism for the remission of their sins? (Acts 2:38) It's important to note that Jesus demonstrated the ability to meet people wherever they were in their lives.

No matter their racial, cultural, or religious background, Jesus knew how to connect with people to accomplish His spiritual purpose for meeting them. (John 4:1-39) Many times Jesus helped people by engaging with them through the development of a social relationship.

Notice a few areas where a relationship with Jesus was obtained but came to fruition through a strong social connection engineered by the Master.

Social Connection

"The two disciples heard him speak, and they followed Jesus. 38 And Jesus turned and saw them following, and said to them, 'What do you seek?' They said to Him, 'Rabbi (which translated means Teacher), where are You staying?"
– John 1:37-38

Jesus was social. Not only was Jesus social, but He also used His social skills to socially connect with people to invest in their discipleship and destiny. When two of John the Baptist's disciples began to follow Jesus, the Lord asked them what they sought. (John 1:38) Jesus encountered men who had already been seeking and searching for the coming Messiah. This is a powerful revelation that gives us a glimpse into the ministry mindset of our

Jesus was social.

Lord. Jesus was keenly aware of what motivated these men and what they sought. He engaged these two men in conversation so they could discover He was indeed the manifestation of their Messianic desires.

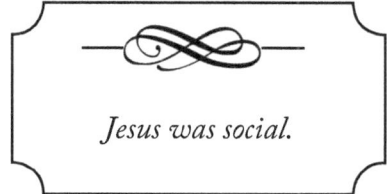

The two disciples asked where Jesus was staying which indicates that they desired an intimate and social relationship. (John 1:38) Where Jesus was staying indicated these men sought personal observation, explication, and acceptance of Jesus upon invitation. Maybe through accompanying Him they concluded they could ask questions, visually observe His behavior in His home and confirm the Messianic authenticity of John's claim of this Jesus truly being the Lamb of God. (John 1:36)

"He said to them, 'Come, and you will see.' So they came and saw where He was staying; and they stayed with Him that day, for it was about the tenth hour."
– John 1:39

Jesus invited two of John's disciples to accompany Him so they could see what they desired and spend time with Him socially. (John 1:39-42) The personality of our Lord and Savior Jesus was such that He was willing to take time to be social with people. Jesus was willing to allow His new disciples to immediately see Him in His comfort zone. He revealed a personal side to His ministry, thus making those who came in contact with Him more knowledgeable of His identity. How awesome was it for Andrew and the other disciple who accompanied him to spend a day with the God of the universe, the King of Kings and Lord of Lords?

The Power of Social Connection

"One of the two who heard John speak and followed Him, was Andrew, Simon Peter's brother. 41 He found first his own brother Simon and said to him, 'We have found the Messiah' (which translated means Christ). 42 He brought him to Jesus. Jesus looked at him and said, 'You are Simon the son of John; you shall be called Cephas' (which is translated, Peter)."
– John 1:40-42

There is so much power, knowledge, and understanding in studying the above passage from an evangelistic purview. Notice after he spent a day with Jesus, of first importance Andrew went and **"found"** his brother Simon. (John 1:41) After following Jesus, Andrew immediately found who was probably his closest relative and family member. Andrew found his own brother first! (John 1:41)

According to John, it was Andrew who helped his brother Simon whom we all know as Peter (Greek name) discover the Lord Jesus. This is the same Simon, Peter who preached the first sermon on the day of Pentecost after the Holy Spirit fell among the apostles when about three thousand souls were baptized into Jesus Christ for the remission of their sins. (Acts 2:1-47) God used Andrew's newly acquired knowledge of the Messiah as a tactical tool to reach his brother Peter, who was himself seeking the Messiah.

The application for the soul winners from John's aforementioned gospel account is to simply **FIND** truth-seekers and **BRING** them to Jesus! (John 1:37-42) Finding and bringing happens after soul winners have experienced an encounter with Jesus Christ and have come to know Him as the Messiah! Christians will become permanently changed for the better after spending quality time with Jesus. The natural sensation after coming to know Jesus is the need to find those in your immediate circle of influence. Finding family members who are seeking to **FIND** an authentic relationship with Jesus is powerfully important in the art of soul winning. It was apparent that the text suggests that Andrew and perhaps Simon were both looking for the Messiah, since Andrew tells his brother, "*We have found the Messiah*". (John 1:41)

It is imperative to note that with His infinite wisdom, Jesus allowed someone to spend some time with Him socially who was searching for the Messiah! As disciples, we need to identify those who want salvation, those who desire knowledge, and people who are searching to find the truth. Soul winners must trust God to divinely orchestrate our paths in the direction of those searching for an authentic relationship with the Lord! Being prepared to notice who has shown interest in the knowledge you have concerning the Messiah is of strategic importance.

Use spiritual discernment to **bring** people into your social circle who desire the information you have about the Messiah. These interactions are what we as soul winners live for! These kinds of divine interactions can occur when biblical content is distributed in both physical and virtual venues! Lost souls are won when they are placed in CONTACT and COMMUNICATION with Jesus Christ our Lord.

Needs-Based Connections

Regardless of what ministries are being conducted, the ultimate goal for EVERY MINISTRY is to bring people to Jesus. Jesus identified that Andrew was seeking to find out if He was truly the Christ. Consequently, the Lord invited Andrew and the other disciple into His personal space to help him gain access to the answers Andrew needed to solidify his faith. After Andrew had completed his confirmation proceedings, he concluded that Jesus was the Messiah, so he **BROUGHT** Simon to Jesus! (John 1:42)

In my ministry, I have learned to identify the needs of people, but always with the intent of ultimately exposing them to an authentic spiritual relationship with Christ Jesus after helping them with their needs. (Matthew 25:31-46) Ministries are not hard to create. Visionary leaders must have the ability to see areas of human need and create ministries that provide aid for those in need. Ministry can indeed become arduous when the results and effectiveness are not forthcoming as planned or hoped for. Needs-based ministries meet the needs of people who may have a specific need that your ministry can help with and provides social opportunities to plant the seed of the word of God into willing hearers.

Mission over Condition

"Therefore, those who had been scattered went about preaching the word."
– Acts 8:4

The 1st century Christians in Jerusalem clearly understood that the mission of saving souls superseded their adverse conditions. Being persecuted and scattered as a result of following Christ did not discourage these Christians from their mission. (Acts 8:4) They remained connected to their mission. Unfortunately, the global pandemic caused many churches and ministries to surrender to the adverse conditions and stop their missions.

Unfortunately, some churches didn't have the resources or manpower to utilize the available resources to continue their missions. When the doors to the church buildings closed, it resulted in many families closing the doors of their faith. Some families who were primarily accustomed to the spiritual routine of physically assembling on Sunday allowed their worship of God as well as their mission work to evaporate.

Many Christians failed to make the adjustments by transitioning to a safer home method via the internet to continue their spiritual mission because they allowed the condition of the Coronavirus to supersede God's mission. Soul winning is a mission that must take place regardless of the condition in the world. God needs purpose-driven missionaries and creative innovators that will not allow the rudimentary principles of spreading the gospel to be thwarted. We need soul winners like the men and woman of God in Acts 8:4 who knew their mission and carried it out regardless of the peril and adverse conditions which faced them. The difference between being on the verge of a BREAKDOWN or a BREAKTHROUGH is what Christians allow the PRESSURES and adversities of life to PRODUCE.

The Art of Soul Winning is ammunition from God for all ministers, pastors, leaders, clergy, and ministry workers to have a blueprint to continue to do effective ministry as well as save souls during adverse conditions. The social media age presents a plethora of problems and issues because of the state of mankind and its vices. However, God has blessed soul winners with the creative abilities to be strategically resourceful, successful, and fruitful in the mission of saving souls despite our conditions. Will you become a part of the strategic solutions to aid in populating Heaven?

Messages of Hope

The Coronavirus pandemic taught me much about creativity when leading a congregation while the doors to the church building were shut. In the words of one preacher, I decided to turn the PANDEMIC into a PLAN-DEMIC! One of the lessons I learned was the reality that everyone needs real hope! So many people either contracted the virus or had family members diagnosed with it. Unfortunately, many people had members who perished from it. People were constantly seeking to connect and desperately in need of hope.

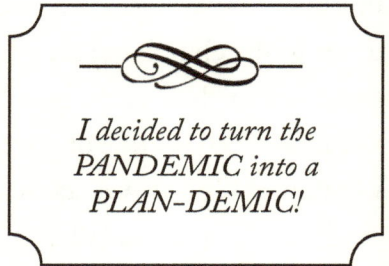

> *I decided to turn the PANDEMIC into a PLAN-DEMIC!*

The Lord gave me the idea to produce videos of people in my local congregation who had overcome enormous adversities. We shared those testimonial videos with the world on virtual and social media platforms. People who made it through heart transplants, surgeries, coronavirus, grief, divorce, bad relationships, were cured of cancer and drug addictions all had an opportunity to share their success stories through their testimonies which we called "Messages of Hope".

This ministry did several positive things. It met the need of providing people hope and it glorified God for being a Healer and a Miracle Worker with proof from members who experienced God's miraculous blessings.

This video series also allowed us to get members involved in coordinating the video series. It gave those who gave testimonies a chance to share what God did privately in their lives to help other people publicly.

The content in these videos reached people who were devoid of an authentic relationship with Jesus Christ. Placing these videos on social media gave us a wider viewing audience that would find our "Messages of Hope" instrumental to their own lives. Thus, the Messages of Hope series provided hope for individuals who had never entered our physical church building. When soul winners see the big picture of ministry connecting with the human experience, it provides precious opportunities to preach the gospel of Jesus Christ to the lost!

Needs-based ministries help people by providing aid for their needs. God gives believers a bi-vocational ability to help with humanity's needs which also gives us a chance to spread the gospel to those whose needs we meet. The Lord blessed us to conduct several ministries during a very dismal season for many families and this provided enormous encouragement to people in need.

During some of those ministry opportunities we looked up several times and saw that the local news stations came to televise what God was doing in our ministry. This exposed thousands of people to the great things the Lord was doing with our mission. Remember, God must open hearts, and those hearts need a place to develop and grow. That special place should be with your church's ministry! Ministry is about connecting Jesus to people who need Him.

CHAPTER 8

STRATEGY #7: USE GIFTED AND TALENTED SPIRITUAL PEOPLE

I'm fully aware that many people take the position that the church is the place where people should receive opportunities to use their gifts. That statement could and should be true if those individuals were committed to consistently demonstrating spirituality and regular practice to improve in their gifts. Then, opportunities to use those practiced gifts would make sense, but certainly notwithstanding efforts to be skilled in a particular area of interest. The church isn't a playground or an experimentation stage.

> *The church isn't a playground or an experimentation stage.*

Most of us wouldn't dare take a loved one to a hospital that didn't have verifiable medical credentials. Unless it was an emergency, I don't know anyone who would give the hospital's attendants, nurses, and doctors the approval to help a loved one without them having any credentials, training, or the biological acumen to successfully treat your family members. If the church is a hospital for the spiritually sick, the same expectation of trained spiritual professionals should apply to the Lord's church as it would a regular hospital.

We live in an age where Christians desire titles to lead ministries before they accept a tenable theology, develop teaching ability, display spiritual talent, or possess the tenacity to live righteously. Too many leaders have ruined vibrant church ministries because they placed people in positions for the wrong reasons which were devoid of spirituality. It is dangerous to give ministerial leadership positions to people because of popularity, social influence, familial legacy, and church politics. Sadly, these decisions are often made by leaders who know that the people they placed in ministerial leadership roles never displayed the spiritual growth necessary to be an example to lead others.

Skill

"So Saul said to his servants, 'Provide for me now a man who can play well and bring him to me.' 18 Then one of the young men said, 'Behold, I have seen a son of Jesse the Bethlehemite who is a skillful musician, a mighty man of valor, a warrior, one prudent in speech, and a handsome man; and the LORD is with him.' 19 So Saul sent messengers to Jesse and said, 'Send me your son David who is with the flock.'"
– 1 Samuel 16:17-19

When Saul the King needed someone to play an instrument for him to soothe his spirit, he didn't just request someone who could play an instrument. Saul requested an individual who could play the instrument well. (1 Samuel 16:17) This demand ultimately culminated in the King requesting the services of David. David came to Saul to avail his skill after a young man verbally confessed that he was visually aware of David's skillful musicianship which would undoubtedly satisfy the King's demands. (1 Samuel 16:17)

Though David possessed many wonderful attributes, the attribute of his skillful musicianship was in demand. Being skilled in one area of need by the King allowed him to have all his attributes noted. (1 Samuel 16:17-19) It is also interesting to note that when you are skilled, one doesn't have to necessarily go looking for opportunities. Saul specifically and intentionally sent for David because probably unbeknownst to David, someone had been watching him display his skill. The wisdom literature teaches us that a man's gift will make room for him and place him in the company of great men. (Proverbs 16:7)

Zeal is absolutely important and great, but too many ministries die with people who have zeal and no skill. In my estimation, one of the biggest detractors from the development of a highly successful ministry occurs when people who haven't developed the skill or the desire to improve are thrust into the spotlight. Without the necessary training, giftedness, or spiritual drive to improve their craft, being thrust into situations unprepared can be detrimental for all parties involved. No matter how much a person desires to work in an area, skill and spirituality are needed.

> *Zeal is absolutely important and great, but too many ministries die with people who have zeal and no skill.*

Whether singing, preaching, publicly reading scripture, praying, reading announcements, greeting, conducting evangelism, or leading, all areas in ministry require a skill. Your skill in preaching or singing will not outweigh the life you live. Living an unrighteous life will always darken the light of the usefulness of your gift. Life overshadows your gift so make sure your life is in harmony with your spiritual gift.

The Vision to Help people

Evangelism is an art. Art always gets better with practice, desire, creativity, attention to detail, and doing the small things that make a big difference. The Lord requires all disciples to win souls, but without training, desire, and improvement, one can easily run souls away from the protective spiritual custody of the Lord. Soul winners of necessity need to be equipped with the skills to help people.

The goal of evangelism is to help people by bringing them into a saved relationship with Jesus. This reality often comes to fruition when God gives the preachers, evangelists, the man of God, or ministers a vision to do so. In Acts 16:9 it is interesting to note WHO the Lord gave the vision to so those who needed spiritual help received it.

"A vision appeared to Paul in the night: a man of Macedonia was standing and appealing to him, and saying, 'Come over to Macedonia and help us.'"
– Acts 16:9

The preacher to whom the vision APPEARED

The vision to help people appeared to Paul who was a preacher, apostle, and teacher of the gospel of Christ. (1 Timothy 2:7) Paul was also a tent maker by trade. (Acts 18:1-3) Paul **RECEIVED** the vision that God gave him in the night and **IMMEDIATELY RESPONDED TO THE URGENCY OF THE VISION** given by God. (Acts 16:9-10; 18:9) Make no mistake, because of who he is, God has given the man of God a unique perspective in his skillset and gifts to be utilized for God's kingdom agenda.

As the Lord did for Israel with the assignment of Moses to lead God's people, God does the same with the evangelist through his assignment to spread the gospel of Jesus Christ. God has purposefully given the evangelist, the man of God, an assignment to accomplish His will by furnishing the world with a man, a ministry, and a mission to save souls. (Exodus 3:7-10; 1 Timothy 6:11) God allows vision to appear to those distinctively prepared to carry that vision out by any spiritual means necessary.

Though God gave Paul, the evangelist, a vision to help people, it was the man of God's responsibility to communicate that vision to other faithful disciples to help carry out God's vision. What hurts many evangelism teams and ministries is when the people of God are envious and jealous of who God gave the vision to instead of being thankful that God allows them to be a part of the same vision.

When trying to win souls, each person has a role and responsibility. Differing roles shouldn't be cause for DIVISION. When there is DIVISION, the emphasis is taken away from the VISION of saving souls and using our gifts. Leaders must build passionately driven teams who understand the focus is not just about who decides the logistics of the destination. The destination and purpose of the mission itself are to reach the intended goal. Notice some of the fascinating principles we find from the people who were a part of the vision. (Acts 16:10)

The people who were A PART of the vision

"When he had seen the vision, immediately we sought to go into Macedonia, concluding that God had called us to preach the gospel to them." **Acts 16:10**

- Paul **ARTICULATED** the vision the Lord gave him to the disciples who were with him. (Acts 16:9-10)

- The disciples who were with Paul **URGENTLY RESPONDED** to Paul's vision to help people. (Acts 16:10)

- The disciples who were with Paul **CONSIDERED** themselves a part of Paul's vision to help people. (Acts 16:10)

- The disciples who were with Paul **COMMITTED** themselves to Paul's vision to help people. (Acts 16:10)

- The disciples who were with Paul **CONNECTED** themselves to Paul's vision to help people. (Acts 16:10)

- The disciples who were with Paul **SOUGHT** after the vision to help people. (Acts16:10)

- The disciples who were with Paul **FAITHFULLY TRAVELED** with him to help people. (Acts 16:10)

- The disciples who were with Paul defined **HELP** from Paul's vision as **GOSPEL PREACHING.**

- The disciples who were with Paul **CONCLUDED** that **God CALLED THEM** to be a part of the vision to help people. (Acts 16:10)

- The disciples who were with Paul **BELIEVED** that **PREACHING THE GOSPEL** was a part of the vision to help people. (Acts 16:10)

Pursuing the purposeful vision of winning souls for Jesus is rewarding beyond written or verbal articulation. It is extraordinarily motivating for soul winners when the pitiful predicament of the spiritually needy who are hungry and desperate for truth is brought to light. (Acts 16:9) Notice the spiritual desperation of humanity given to Paul through the vision he received from God. (Acts 16:9)

The people who APPEALED to Paul through the vision

"A vision appeared to Paul in the night: a man of Macedonia was standing and appealing to him, and saying, 'Come over to Macedonia and help us.'"
– Acts 16:9

- The people of Macedonia who appealed to Paul **needed help**. (Acts 16:9)

- Those who appealed to Paul in the dream were **standing and appealing** which usually indicates urgency, seriousness, staunch invocation, or approval for much-needed help. (Acts 16:9)

- The vision given by God to Paul indicated that **men were pleading and appealing for help**. One with vision should concur that when men articulate their need for help and spiritual guidance, they truly need help.

- The people of Macedonia needed someone to help them by **coming to their geographic location**. (Acts 16:9; Mark 16:15)

- Some of the people of Macedonia were **worshippers, entrepreneurs who sold commerce, and willing listeners**. Nevertheless, they were devoid of the spiritual substance a relationship with Jesus Christ provides. (Acts 16:14-15; 30-34)

- **The Lord opened the Macedonian's hearts to respond** to the gospel message when those who received the vision worked together to carry out the vision of the mission. (Acts 16:14-15)

The most effective soul winning teams and ministries understand the power of contributing to the MISSION! Souls will be saved when Christians become CONNECTED to the VISION to HELP PEOPLE! When soul winners have connected with the vision, they **INVEST** and **INVITE** by traveling the distance, putting forth the effort, and being present when needed to make a difference! Use social media, your social mentality, and any social means necessary to arbitrarily help build relationships with sinners. Soul winners are ambassadors for the Lord Jesus Christ who contribute to the MISSION by working together to accomplish a common goal.

Visionary Leaders Train Soul Winners

"And He gave some as apostles, and some as prophets, and some as evangelists, and some as pastors and teachers, 12 for the equipping of the saints for the work of service, to the building up of the body of Christ;"
– Ephesians 4:11-12

The preacher, evangelist, minister, or man of God is a uniquely gifted individual in his role. The evangelist has not only been called by God to spread the good news, he's been called and charged to train others to do the work of ministry as well. (Ephesians 4:12; 2 Timothy 4:1-5) The evangelist has been charged with the specific purpose of "equipping" the saints. (Ephesians 4:12) This means an evangelist must have the skill to build relationships so he is capable of equipping God's people.

Winning souls requires relationship-building to perpetuate the process of developing disciples with the intended purpose of building the body of Christ. (Ephesians 4:12) To "**equip**" simply means to "**prepare**" for a purpose with reaching that end in mind. However, as one man, the evangelist can only build one relationship at a time, but all those whom he equips can constantly build relationships to reach more people. All the weight of servicing the needs of God's people shouldn't fall solely on the evangelist.

The preacher has to be a visionary leader with the ability to see things beyond face value. The man of God must be so acquainted with God's word that he knows what to do in a multiplicity of situations. Because of his thorough handle of scripture, he trains individuals who have faithfully proven they are committed to the work of service. Those whom he successfully trains serve and sustain people through their work. Preachers as visionary leaders matter because we know that where there is no vision, people perish. (Proverbs 29:18)

Church Resurrection

One of the saddest things many of us have witnessed in the social media and technology age is dying churches. When churches are dying their leadership and membership constituents usually don't have the vision to recognize that they are in fact dying. Consequently, they continue the same systems and strategies they once used in their glory days to no avail. Many of these churches never realize that they are like a hamster on a wheel, moving, but going nowhere.

> *Many of these churches never realize that they are like a hamster on a wheel, moving, but going nowhere.*

The social media age has fostered what should be an undeniable reality. The reality is that social media and technology can not only be useful, but they can also save your ministry if the doors to the church building ever become closed. Visionary leaders must see trends, progression, and stagnation to lead in a way that avoids making mistakes detrimental to the future success of the organization.

Leaders have to be acquainted with how business professionals, schools, and progressive, forward-minded people see the culture progressing. Understanding how the movers, shakers, and decision-makers in society receive, respond, and resonate with information is critical for a visionary leader. A visionary must consider how to package information effectively to those they are trying to reach.

Unfortunately, many leaders have failed to see this shift with the youth, kids, teenagers, and young adults in their churches. The younger generation is most likely current with the knowledge to reach people through modern technology and social media. They can also teach the church current methodologies to reach the masses and become actively involved in a ministry doing those very things. Therefore, getting the youth involved in doing kingdom work provides the potentiality for them to have a generational impact. Leaders must be honest in evaluating their ministries as well as committed to doing what needs to be done to effect change to reach the lost.

Observation, honesty, willingness to make strategic adjustments, and the ability to maximize all the available talent before the inevitable shift occurs in ministry is a gift that most visionary leaders possess. All successful ministries utilize effective strategies to win souls in the social media age. Having the vision to notice shifts and trends is paramount. Adaptability in methodology could lead to the consistency of an attractive ministry.

Therefore, the saying, "good preachers aren't cheap and cheap preachers aren't good" is apropos. Leaders with spiritual foresight who possess the ability to grow, teach, train, and administer progressive biblical change to progressively move people are truly gifted men of God. Men who labor at preaching and teaching the word of God to save and sustain souls in the church are worthy of their wages because of their outstanding gifts, spiritual leadership, and labor. (1 Corinthians 9:14; Galatians 6:6)

Purpose

Despite adversity, soul winners must always be committed to purposefully pursuing lives filled with Godly purpose, even in a global pandemic. Nothing matters in Christianity if souls don't matter to the people who are supposed to believe all souls matter! The purpose of visionary leaders, ministry workers, disciples, and laypersons is to **save** and **sustain souls**.

Most all things have a purpose. God always has a purpose so Christians must consistently have a purpose. The devil has a purpose, animals have a purpose, the earth has a purpose, every created thing has a purpose. Diseases have a purpose, people have purposes, righteousness has a purpose and sin has a purpose. Since everything has a purpose, the key for humanity is to keep the opposing adversarial purposes from destroying your Godly purpose.

Purpose in adversity

Notice what the apostle Paul wrote to the church at Rome in Romans 8:28 to give them hope amid their sufferings. There are three distinctions in this verse that provide hope for the believer.

"And we know that God causes all things to work together for good to those who love God, to those who are called according to purpose."
– Romans 8:28

"And we know ..." | **Spiritual Information**

"...that God causes all things to work together for good" | **Sovereign Innovation**

"to those who love God, to those who are called according to His purpose."
| **Sanctified Integration**

It's clear that suffering believers must have an intellectual awareness of **spiritual information**. Without being informed of the spiritual hope that exists with God, the enemy can purposefully steal your hope through his demonic influence. The text of Romans 8:28 doesn't suggest that God causes evil, it means that God is the Causal Being who works all things together for good. (Romans 8:28)

God innovatively causes "all things", both good and the bad to work together for good through His **Sovereign innovation**. This is according to His will, not necessarily the good each individual desires. Through the process of **sanctified integration**, the Lord exclusively works all things together for good to His people who love Him and understand they are called according to His purpose. (Romans 8:28) The word "**purpose**" is defined as a pre-arranged specific passion to pursue and accomplish said goal.

Sometimes God reveals our need to reestablish our purpose through the pain. The Lord will show us that there are hidden blessings in pain that produce the "fruit" of purpose. Many of us have experienced pain from our own or someone else's mistakes. However, mistakes can lead to opportunities to give positive messages as preventative measures in hopes that others don't experience the pain of

> *Sometimes God reveals our need to restablish our purpose through the pain.*

the mistakes we've made. Purposeful messages can cause those who have made mistakes to become motivated to improve.

The **motivation** from hearing a message after making mistakes can lead one to movement. The **movement** from your motivation after hearing a message when you made a mistake, can cause a miracle. **Miracles** lead to **testimonies** that give **God glory**! It all starts with the spiritual and intellectual need to fulfill your purpose. Desire is inextricably linked to motivation, so the desire to fulfill your purpose should make you wake up each day motivated to fulfill your purpose daily.

Read Romans 8:28 | What **two** principles are found in this passage that distinguish the people for whom God allows all things to work together for good?

_____

_____

_____

_____

_____

How can those two sanctified principles give you hope if you do them?

_____

_____

_____

_____

_____

Read Ephesians 2:10 | What name does God use to refer to His people in this passage? What are the Lord's people created for in this passage?

_____

_____

_____

_____

_____

What will you specifically do differently each day as a result of the God-given purposes you've read about in Romans 8:28 and Ephesians 2:10?

_____

_____

_____

_____

_____

Passion

Passion is a feeling of intense enthusiasm or a compelling desire for someone or something. Passion can range from eager interest or admiration for an idea, proposal, or cause; to enthusiastic enjoyment of an interest or activity; to strong attraction, excitement, or emotion towards a person. As an emotion, passion can't be taught, but passion can be developed. Through experiences and exposures, God uses passion to motivate soul winners to possess their passion to save the lost.

Gifted leaders and visionaries must have passion, a strong compelling, intense emotion for implementing strategies for winning souls in the social media age. Leaders are wise to understand the importance of passionately saving those who will die without a relationship with Jesus Christ. Passionate soul winners are trained to help those who fail to understand that eternal punishment or pleasure lies ahead in mankind's future. A leader's passion alone can become the driving force a ministry needs as congregants and constituents tend to encapsulate and ingratiate the personality and purpose of the Minister into their own lives.

"The things which you have heard from me in the presence of many witnesses, entrust these to faithful men who will be able to teach others also."
– 2 Timothy 2:2

In the apostle Paul's pastoral appeal to his protégé Timothy, he instructed the young evangelist to teach what Timothy had learned from Paul. Timothy was told to teach what he learned from Paul to faithful men who had the skill and giftedness to teach others. (2 Timothy 2:2) In his statement, Paul specifically and intentionally wanted Timothy to target men who had demonstrated themselves faithful. The specifics of Paul's instruction extended to those who possessed the kind of teaching ability that would resonate with other people. As an application, seek to mass duplicate teachers with accurate biblical education, information, righteousness, and ability. The preservation and transformation of the next generation of soul winners will largely be impacted by their indoctrination!

STUDY GUIDE

Leadership

Before one can lead anyone, they must become a learned follower, a disciple of the One to whom they are following. Notice the summons of discipleship that Jesus taught His disciples and others about the requirements to come after Him.

"And He summoned the crowd with His disciples, and said to them, 'If anyone wishes to come after Me, he must deny himself, and take up his cross and follow Me.'"
– Mark 8:34

- **Sincere Desire** | "If anyone wishes to come after Me…"
- **Spiritual Dedication** | *"he must…"*
- **Self-Denial** | *"deny himself…"*
- **Sacrificial Discipline** | *"and take up his cross"*
- **Servant Discipleship** | *"and follow Me."*

In His instructional teaching, Jesus emphasized how deep internal convictions concerning Him would lead to an external demonstration of commitment to Him.

Read Mark 8:34: Notice how the instruction of Jesus did not capitulate to external distractions, but internal convictions. How should this affect your view of discipleship? What should it change?

_____

_____

_____

There are typically two types of leadership, **role, and real leadership**. *Role leadership* is positional, transactional or categorical, but doesn't necessarily encompass any Christological attributes. ***Real leadership*** occurs when Christian servanthood is demonstrated and God's will is modeled by His servants. (Matthew 23:1-7; 23:11; Mark 8:38)

What areas will you improve upon or strengthen to lead others as you follow Christ?

_____

_____

_____

_____

_____

CHAPTER 9

"A Disobedient Child with a Compassionate God."
– Jonah 1:1-4; 17

Sometimes people believe they are called to ministry but have reservations about their calling. Many Christians remain unsure about what God's intentions are for them and what God wants them to do. Let it be known that God calls all disciples of Christ to preach the gospel to win the lost. (Mark 16:15-16; Acts 8:1-4)

There is a man in God's word who was called by God to save souls but struggled with his calling. The prophet is named Jonah and he rebelled against following God's instructions. (Jonah 1:1-3) God called Jonah to relay a prophetic message to the wicked sinners of Nineveh to turn from their wicked ways to avoid God's impending destruction. (Jonah 1:1-3; 3:4) Maybe Jonah's story can shed some light to provide some spiritual clarity, motivation, and direction to obey God's instructions to save souls. I believe there is a soul winner deep in your soul that God wants to reveal to the world! Let God use you!

Although there have been countless critics and numerous attacks on its content, the book of Jonah is arguably one of the most fascinating books to read not only in the Old Testament but throughout the entirety of the biblical canon. Though it is named after the 8th-century prophet Jonah, its content is not about Jonah, it's about the God of Jonah. The revelation of the Lord's *communication, commission, and compassion* for Jonah and the wicked people of Nineveh gives readers a fascinating glimpse into the mind of God.

These poignant pages of inspiration in this historical narrative have become a paramount reflection of the Sovereign God of Israel's awareness, attention, and responsive action towards sin, human frailties, grace, disobedience, destruction, deliverance, and salvation. The book of Jonah can literally be summed up in one word, **compassion**, which is the Lord's sympathetic pity and concern for one's misfortunes. One of the more interesting occurrences in human history takes place in this Old Testament minor prophet book of Jonah which has proven to be theologically tenable throughout time.

Communication

"The word of the LORD came to Jonah the son of Amittai saying,
'Arise, go to Nineveh the great city and cry against it, for their
wickedness has come up before Me.'"
– Jonah 1:1-2

The word of the Lord was communicated to Jonah, the son of Amittai, an 8th century BC prophet. (Jonah 1:1) The transmission of Jonah's mission was unmistakably communicated through God's word presumably by inspiration, solidifying God's commission for Jonah to preach to the Ninevites to seek their repentance. As recorded in Jonah 1:2, Nineveh was the "great city", the capital of Assyria, now modern-day Iraq, close in a geographic location to Mosul, east of the Tigris river, 550 miles northeast of Samaria.

The narrative of Jonah distinguishes the behavior of the people of Nineveh as wicked and violent (Jonah 1:2; 3:8). The Ninevites also worshiped idol gods of love and war. They committed violent atrocities against humanity and harlotry was perpetually rampant among the population of more than 120,000 persons whose hearts were devoid of spiritual acumen. The people of Nineveh were those whose documented actions proved they possessed no moral compass. (Jonah 4:11)

Commission

"The word of the LORD came to Jonah the son of Amittai saying,
"Arise, go to Nineveh the great city and cry against it, for their
wickedness has come up before Me."
–Jonah 1:1-2

The substance of the text theologically teaches how God commissioned Jonah by calling him to save the lost people of Nineveh (Jon 1:1-2) Interestingly, in like manner, God also commissioned Christian believers to save the lost people even today in modernity. We discover the process of the commission and calling of Jonah in verses one and two. God called a **leader** (Jonah), God gave the **leader a lesson** (arise, go), God gave the **leader a lesson and a location** (Nineveh) and God demonstrated His **love** (saving wicked people). It becomes clear that God's intended purpose was to use a "called person" to save "lost persons".

After reading these four short chapters, if one performs behavioral exegesis on Jonah's rebellion toward his commission, it becomes quite clear that God doesn't call the qualified, He qualifies those whom He calls. For the Christian readers who are digesting the depth of this declaration let's be clear, SAVING LOST PEOPLE IS WHAT GOD HAS CALLED YOU TO DO! Then the question becomes, HOW SHOULD I RESPOND WHEN GOD CALLS ME TO SAVE THE LOST?

Notice two requirements for those who have received God's commission and desire to adopt His commission as your mission.

GOD'S COMMISSION REQUIRES AN IMMEDIATE RESPONSE

"But Jonah rose up to flee to Tarshish from the presence of the LORD. So he went down to Joppa, found a ship which was going to Tarshish, paid the fare, and went down into it to go with them to Tarshish from the presence of the LORD."
– Jonah 1:3

God's commission required Jonah to "arise and go" because God is indeed a God of not an only assignment, but action. We can safely speculate that the majority of persons living in the 21st century are acutely aware of communication devices since we use cell phones for calls and texts, emails and instant messages. And we are aware of the urgency with which people expect a timely reply in response to our acts of communication. God is no different. His calling requires ACTION as an acceptable response with a sense of urgency as well.

Just as people respond to communications quickly to receive favor and *obtain blessings*, we must also respond with rapidity to the Lord's instructions when receiving communication, no matter what the assignment or who we are assigned to save. Obeying His commands brings *blessings*. Nonetheless, many people have prolonged the inevitable by refusing to move in the direction the Lord has commanded. Jonah was one of those people. After being commissioned he rose up, but journeyed in the opposite direction of the Lord's commission. (Jonah 1:3)

GOD'S COMMISSION REQUIRES A FAITHFUL RESPONSE

Jonah was specifically commissioned by God to *"arise, go to Nineveh the great city"*, but Jonah's GPS navigation system took him on a detour to Tarshish! It appears Jonah was not pleased with his new job description so instead of tendering his two weeks' notice, Jonah decided to quit. Jonah's response to God was an unfaithful one as he responded by rising and heading in the opposite direction of Nineveh as God requested. (Jonah 1:2) Jonah went to Joppa and found a ship there which was destined to go an estimated 2500 miles west to Tarshish.

The text teaches us that Jonah was trying to flee from the presence of the Lord. (Jonah 1:3) I'm not sure about you, but the last time I checked, God was omnipotent, omniscient, and omnipresent which means that the possibility of escaping God's presence is absolutely, unequivocally zero. You can't escape God's presence, but people try it.

This is not the first time mankind tried to flee from the presence of God as there is a biblical commonality concerning this reality. After Adam and Eve ate of the forbidden tree of the knowledge of good and evil they became intellectually aware of their nakedness, felt ashamed, and attempted to hide from the presence of the Lord among the trees of the garden. (Genesis 3:8) Another instance occurred after Cain killed Abel, Cain went out from the presence of the Lord. (Genesis 4:16)

In contrast, King David was a man who was after God's own heart. He knew the value of being in the presence of the Lord. The wisdom literature of the Psalmist recorded these words from David, "Do not cast me away from your presence And do not take Your Holy Spirt from me." (Psalm 51:11) When mankind attempts to leave the presence of God because of disobedience, one leaves much to be desired. Woven within the tapestry of the presence of the Lord is not only God's PRESENCE, but also His PROVISION, POWER, PROTECTION, and PROMISES. A heart of disobedience leaves God's presence, but a heart of obedience remains in God's presence!

As you read this your mind may become reflective of personal instances where you neglected to respond faithfully to God's commissioning in your life. With that reality, one can easily reflect on the cost of those decisions. Notice what refusing to comply with God's instructions to save the people of Nineveh and his attempt to flee from the presence of the Lord cost Jonah.

The Cost of an Unfaithfulness Response

- Jonah wasted both EMOTIONAL and PHYSICAL ENERGY by deliberately attempting to flee from the presence of the Lord. | **Jonah 1:3**

- Jonah wasted TIME by deliberately attempting to flee from the presence of the Lord. | **Jonah 1:3**

- Jonah found a SHIP headed in the wrong direction of the Lord's commissioned destination by deliberately attempting to flee from the presence of the Lord. | **Jonah 1:3**

- Jonah wasted MONEY by deliberately attempting to flee from the presence of the Lord. | **Jonah 1:3**

- Jonah BOARDED onto a ship to assemble with people who were headed in the opposite direction of God's assignment by deliberately attempting to flee from the presence of the Lord. | **Jonah 1:3**

Compassion

"The LORD hurled a great wind on the sea and there was a great storm on the sea so that the ship was about to break up."
– Jonah 1:4

Because he attempted to flee from the presence of the Lord after he boarded a ship headed in the opposite direction of God's instructions, Jonah finds himself in a storm, one of catastrophic proportions. (Jonah 1:4) It is here that the Lord reveals to the reader of this historical narrative His nature to demonstrate compassion to those in relationship with Him. The Hebrew word for compassion is חוס which is translated as the word "chus". This verb, compassion, is mentioned twice in Jonah 4:10-11 and is defined as sympathetic pity and concern for one's misfortunes.

Although the word compassion is only mentioned twice in chapter four of the book of Jonah, God demonstrates this compassion through His actions throughout the entirety of the narrative. What becomes fascinating is the method God used to distribute His compassion towards Jonah.

GOD DEMONSTRATES HIS COMPASSION WHEN HE CAUSES A STORM

"The LORD hurled a great wind on the sea and there was a great storm on the sea so that the ship was about to break up."
– Jonah 1:4

God demonstrated His compassion to Jonah through a great storm. (Jonah 1:4) Interestingly, it is typically antithetical to associate a storm with God's compassion, but the Lord reveals a powerful principle in Jonah 1:4 that is pregnant with relative truth concerning mankind's anthropological history of disobeying His instructions. This narratological discourse informs us that sometimes it's not the devil that is causing the storms, it's the LORD causing a storm to demonstrate His compassion! When a called individual disobeys God, refusing to submit to His calling, one method God uses is to allow storms in that person's life.

God never intended for Jonah to be on that ship headed to Tarshish, but what we find woven in this passage is the fact that if God cannot change the heart of that individual, the Lord will CHANGE the atmospheric conditions (great wind/storms) to change the individual's direction. The same God who calmed the sea when He spoke to it is the same God who can weaponize the sea to halt and hinder disobedient movements, enforcing travel restrictions.

The LORD demonstrated His ability to change and rearrange situations through a great storm when God isn't successful in His attempts to change your mind. Though the ship hadn't broken up at the point of the tornadic storm, it was well on its way to breaking up. The principle is that there are metaphoric ships in everyone's life that God has the power and prerogative to "break up" if those to whom He has commissioned are rebellious to His intended calling for their lives.

Another glaring principle in the text is many people will remain rebellious until they are forced to change or have no other options. This mindset is critically dangerous because it suggests that when some people have OPTIONS, they tend to be complacent, prolonging the inevitable, as complacency is the enemy of ACTION, ACTIVITIES, and AGGRESSION. When God wants His people to move, but they are reluctant, God has a historical track record of removing their OPTIONS so that His people have no choice but to comply with God's selected course of action.

In the year 2020, the global Coronavirus (COVID-19) pandemic claimed hundreds of thousands of lives. By God allowing the pandemic to occur, it was a clear indication of how God uses such opportunities to get people to DO what they were previously complacent in doing when options were available. Those who deserted God for selfish reasons, money, and other priorities finally came to grips that they needed God's presence when their options were stripped, finding themselves quarantined in their homes with nothing to do but pray to God for help as Jonah did (Jonah 2:1). An adequate application appropriate in response to this principle is to simply become obedient before you have your options taken away due to a lack of spiritual movement. Having options has always been an example of God's Grace.

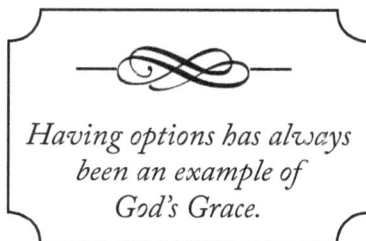

> *Having options has always been an example of God's Grace.*

GOD DEMONSTRATES HIS COMPASSION WHEN HE CARES FOR YOU DURING A STORM

"And the LORD appointed a great fish to swallow Jonah, and Jonah was in the stomach of the fish three days and three nights."
– Jonah 1:17

Jonah was confident that God's compassion would result in Him calming the very storm that He caused if Jonah removed himself as a passenger on the ship, thus saving the other passengers from storm-related deaths. Having a dual purpose of attempted suicide and a rescue plan for those accompanying Jonah on the ship, Jonah asked the innocent passengers to throw him overboard. (Jonah 1:11-12; 15) However, the Lord once again demonstrated His compassion for Jonah by caring for him during his storm.

Sometimes the real reason why we go through these storms is not that God is trying to punish us, but because He is trying to PROTECT us, to save us from ourselves, keeping us in His presence, provisions, power, promises, and protective custody even during our disobedience! The Lord appointed a great fish, which many scholars believe to be a sperm whale, to swallow, not to eat or chew him, but to save him. (Jonah 1:17) It's evident that if God was able to appoint a great fish and the fish had enough sense to obey the Lord, surely every person in the world should!

In Jonah 1:17 we see God's **protection** (swallowed by great fish), God's **patience** (compassion with disobedience), and God's **purpose** (Jonah's repentance/Jonah's proclamation/Nineveh's repentance). Although Jonah was ANOINTED, his behavior was consistently ANNOYING! However, we can all learn how compassionate God is when what we thought was the Lord's punishment was actually His PREPARATION. What we think is a PENALTY is really His PROTECTION! When God ultimately has a calling over your life, He can still demonstrate care for you even when you don't deserve it.

Jonah's destiny was connected to God, but he avoided the Holy One who could help him. God gave him a storm to get him to restrict his movement in the opposite direction of his Godly destiny. Jonah had to be quarantined, isolated in the stomach of the great fish, a dark place for three days and nights before he finally realized through contemplation and prayer what a compassionate God he served, and obedience was his best option! (Jonah 2:1-10) Sometimes we, too, must find ourselves in that nasty, disgusting, uncomfortable dark place before we realize obedience to our communication and commission to God is the best response to such a compassionate God's providential care.

Since the fall of mankind in the garden of Eden with Adam and Eve and throughout man's anthropological existence, evil has consistently spoken. But evangelism has been silent in recent years among modern evangelicals. Just as the gruesome atrocities and crimes against humanity by the Ninevites pained the heart of Jonah, our current cultural climate in

America boasts the same atrocities against humanity. It pains our hearts to witness the senseless loss of too many lives in the African American community.

The world we live in today is one big Nineveh! So today, God needs a Jonah in every country. God needs a Jonah in every city, a Jonah in every community, a Jonah on every corner, and a Jonah in every church. The world won't repent until someone comes preaching the Name of Jesus Christ, our Risen Savior, our Redeeming and Reigning King, the Prince of Peace who has the power to forgive sin and turn hearts of hate to hearts of love.

This world is in desperate need of someone who understands that God is not only compassionate with the behavior of those in relationship with Him, but also equally compassionate toward those who need a relationship with God so they can save the wicked from God's wrath as the Ninevites who repented were. (Jonah 3:1-10)

Can God send you? Will you go proclaim the gospel of Jesus Christ to save people whose behavior is abhorrent and despicable? Are you willing to help the lost receive the same level of compassion from God as you received? Or will you keep running like Jonah, going through storm after storm because you hate the thought of God's compassion being distributed on the wicked? Jonah's repentance ultimately led to the wicked Ninevite's repentance and eliminated God's wrath towards the Ninevites. (Jonah 3:1-10)

APPLICATION: Obey the instructions of our compassionate God of Heaven by seeking to save what is lost. Time is running out; lives are at stake.

Time is running out; lives are at stake.

CHAPTER 10

CONCLUSION

In March of 1997, just sixteen days after his own untimely death, the late rapper Notorious B.I.G. released his second and final studio album entitled, "Life After Death". The significance of bringing this to your attention is the fact that even in popular culture, some believe there is, indeed, life after death. We know that scripture has consistently held the position of life after death.

Jesus Christ Himself has been a staunch proponent on the validity of eternal life either in Heaven or hell for the final destination of humanity. For believers, it is not even a question. It is a fact that a faithful relationship with Jesus Christ is the most important thing we have in preparation for a peaceful afterlife. Evangelism for the soul winner is a passionate and fervent desire to populate Heaven and depopulate hell for those who may not be aware of the reality of earthly mortality.

The art of winning souls is the last defense for the souls of mankind. Conducting serious evangelism is the business of preparing souls for their eternal dwellings. Mankind has demonstrated strength in the area of preparing for many things. We prepare for vacations, meetings, interviews, final examinations, sports games, the weekends, savings accounts, 401k's, and trust funds. Many people live life unprepared for the coming of Jesus Christ and their resurrection for life after death. For those of us who are saved by demonstrating faith in Jesus Christ through the obedience of His gospel, we know this eternal reality. We can have comfort knowing we will spend eternity in paradise with the Lord Jesus Christ. (1 Thessalonians 4:15-18)

The soul winner's job is to sound the alarm for the world so that men, women, boys, and girls understand life, sin, life after death, and the coming of Jesus Christ. We do this so that everyone can be adequately equipped and prepared for that day whenever it comes. It is not enough for the soul's winner to be satisfied with your personal salvation. Someone has to go and tell the world about Jesus! Who's going to go do it?

Are you prepared to tell the world about King Jesus in the age of social media, technology, and among the unchurched? Those who are unchurched usually know nothing about how serious being saved from the punishment un-repented sinners will face in the judgment. They need to know God will give an eternal reward for those of faith, but He will separate those without faith in Christ with eternal punishment!

The legendary boxer, Muhammad Ali utilized a unique strategy to become victorious over George Foreman, the overwhelming favorite during their 1974 "Rumble in the Jungle" fight when the odds to win were against Ali. Similarly, the global Coronavirus (Covid-19) pandemic is the 21st century's Rumble in the Jungle fight for Christians. The global and cultural acceptance of sin has also delivered a pulverizing blow to Christian's in the fight to reclaim humanity for Jesus Christ. Sadly, many Christians haven't decided to join the Rumble in the Jungle fight for the salvation of mankind in the sinful jungle of a world we live in. Now, we need effective and proven strategies to win the battle to save souls in the age of social media and technology.

All we need to win the fight for lost souls are teams of uniquely gifted Christians who possess a willingness to implement culturally relevant strategies. If the original salvation army, the Church of Christ, plans to be effective in winning souls for Christ, we must believe God will use our strategic efforts to be successful in populating Heaven. It doesn't matter how big, bad, and ugly our opponents are, we will be victorious in our fight to save lost souls if we strategically change our mentality to utilize new strategies and expand our methodology! We have all the spiritual weaponry we need, it's simply a matter of soul winners using what we already have to win!

> *We have all the spiritual weaponry we need, it's simply a matter of soul winners using what we already have to win!*

This book, *The Art of Soul Winning*, has enough strategies, motivation, and specific direction proven to be tenable to bless you and those in your group who desire to save souls for Christ. Oh, what a day of rejoicing it will be for those of us who gave our lives to Christ when we are reunited in Heaven with one another when this world is no more! We will be grateful for the work, labor, toil, tears and tremendous dedication we put forth! Once this old world is said and done, we will all reside in Heaven!

It is my hope, trust, and everlasting prayer that those who read this book use this information. My desire is that the lessons in these pages help with your journey wherever you are to populate Heaven in the age of social media. This book is most useful as a tool for your soul winning class, evangelism teams, church growth missions, new members, or anyone to use as ammunition to save souls. Don't look solely at results, look at the effective strategies the Lord can use to bless your efforts if you work hard. If you have planted the seed and watered your seed, you have done your job. Work to improve on planting and watering seeds daily and never stop!

BECOMING A CHRISTIAN

Information is powerful. The biblical information God requires for sinners to become authentic Christians is something you will treasure for eternity. Without it, sinners will never have the biblical, spiritual, mental, and emotional security of knowing they have an authentic saved relationship with Jesus Christ according to God's word.

Review the Becoming a Christian information below to educate yourself and understand what's required by God to become a Christian. Jesus died so that everyone in the world could be exposed to the gospel and be saved by His sacrifice. The appropriate biblical response to Jesus'

The appropriate biblical response to Jesus' sacrificial death matters.

sacrificial death matters. If you are a soul winner, teach people what God requires to become a Christian using the scriptures. If you're not a Christian, you need to become a Christian today!

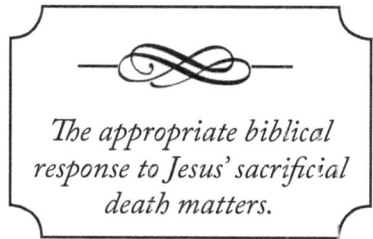

- **Becoming a Christian** requires *hearing* that Jesus Christ died, He was buried, and He rose again from the dead on the third day as a sin Sacrifice for the atonement for your sins according to the scriptures. (1 Corinthians 15:1-4)

- **Becoming a Christian** requires *believing* that Jesus Christ died, He was buried, and He rose from the dead on the third day as a sin Sacrifice for the atonement for your sins according to the scriptures. (Mark 16:15-16; 1 Corinthians 15:1-4)

- **Becoming a Christian** requires a believer to *repent* (a change of mind), resulting from Godly sorrow incurred from past disobedience. (2 Corinthians 7:9-10)

- **Becoming a Christian** requires a believer to *confess* Jesus Christ is both, Lord and Christ, the Son of God. (Acts 2:37; 8:37)

- **Becoming a Christian** requires a believer to be *baptized into Christ* for the remission of sins. (Acts 2:38)

- **Remaining a faithful Christian** requires **a faithful, lifetime commitment to the Lord in His Church** (Hebrews 10:36), *practicing Christianity until death*. (2 Peter 1:5-11; 1 Thessalonians 4:14-18; Revelation 2:10)

**If you want to be baptized and become a Christian, or have some questions concerning salvation, contact the Bryan C. Jones Ministries team at www.bryancjones.com by filling out the Contact Request section or email us at bryancjonesministries@gmail.com

SPECIAL THANKS

Throughout the years God has blessed me by surrounding me with many wonderful family members, loved ones, and friends who have all had an indelible impact on my life. I want to thank my beautiful wife, my mom, friends, professors, and all my preaching mentors for all you've done for me. I also want to thank the many wonderful church members who continue to support my ministry and have prayed for me throughout the years. My journey started and continues to grow because of you all and I am forever grateful for your deposits. May God bless you all.

– Bryan C. Jones

ABOUT THE AUTHOR

Bryan C. Jones serves as the Senior Minister for the Newburg Church of Christ, a dynamic purpose-driven congregation of the Lord's people in Louisville, Kentucky. Bryan is married to Mrs. Danielle P. Jones and in 2018 they published a life-changing dating, relationship, and marriage book entitled *"Finding My Good Thing"* —How God Can Lead You to Your Future Spouse by Dating With a Spiritual Purpose. Bryan is a passionate student of scripture who graduated in December of 2019 with an earned Master's degree in Biblical Studies from Faulkner University in Montgomery, Alabama. Bryan enjoys spending time with his family, traveling, and pursuing his purpose of transforming lives through his life-changing ministry.

BOOKING

To have *The Art of Soul Winning* workshop facilitated at your church or venue, contact the Bryan C. Jones Ministries team at www.bryancjones.com by entering your contact information in the Contact Request section or email us at bryancjonesministries@gmail.com

Bryan C. Jones

MINISTRIES